SOWING PRECIOUS SEED

STORIES OF A NURSE'S SOUL WINNING EXPERIENCES, DESIGNED TO ENCOURAGE CHRISTIANS TO WIN SOULS TO THE SAVIOR

BY
HELEN M. BERRY, R.N.

Copyright © 2010 by HELEN M. BERRY, R.N.

SOWING PRECIOUS SEED
by HELEN M. BERRY, R.N.

Printed in the United States of America

ISBN 9781615796762

All rights reserved solely by the author. The author guarantees all contents are original and do not infringe upon the legal rights of any other person or work. No part of this book may be reproduced in any form without the permission of the author. The views expressed in this book are not necessarily those of the publisher.

Unless otherwise indicated, Bible quotations are taken from King James Version of the Bible.

www.xulonpress.com

May 2012

"Where There is No Vision,
The People Perish."
Prov. 29:18

All Because of Calvary,
Helen Berry

DEDICATION

DEDICATED TO ~
My two sons, Rusty and David Berry,
who gave me unwavering support and confidence
in writing this book. I'm proud of you both
and love you dearly.

Thank you for filling my life with joy—you both
are special gifts that the Lord has given me.

IN LOVING MEMORY OF ~
Marie Hunt ~ My beloved mother. I shall never
forget the sacrifices you made for me. Thank you
for your sweet and godly spirit.

Paul and Annie Lormar ~ My grandparents.
Thank you for the godly example you lived before
me, and for the countless times you prayed for me.

Jane Jones ~ My great-grandmother, who spent
her life as a missionary in Old Wales.
You have made a great, spiritual impact in my life.
What a joy it will be meeting you
for the first time in Heaven.

~ Thank you for giving me a godly heritage ~

ACKNOWLEDGEMENTS

With Special Thanks:

~ To Diane Ward, my gifted editor. Thank you for all your invaluable input and countless hours spent on proofreading and organizing my book for publishing.

~ To Rusty and David Berry, my two sons. Thank you for filling my life with many blessings, and for giving me valuable ideas for my book and book cover. I praise God that He has given me such talented and wonderful children.

~ To Jim and Ann McAlees, my minister and wife. Thank you for your love and kindness to me. Jim, thank you for preaching your heart out every Sunday and for your wealth of knowledge of God's Word. Ann, thank you for your wonderful servant's heart in the little acts of kindness you constantly do for others. You are a real inspiration to me.

~ To Joyce Webster, my precious friend and former minister's wife. Thank you for your sweet fellowship and for the spiritual seeds that you have sown in my life. Thank you for the privilege of being your soul winning partner for so many years. You are a beautiful fragrance in the lives of so many people.

TABLE OF CONTENTS

Introduction xiii
1. First Hand Experience 19
2. Our First Priority 23
3. Follow Me.. 29
4. Objections to the Gospel... 35
5. An Entire Family Won to Christ.............................. 47
6. Get Out of Your Comfort Zone................................ 51
7. Are You Adaptable?.. 56
8. Unusual Plans 63
9. A Lesson from the Flower 69
10. What are you Addicted to? 74
11. Lord, Give Me More Elsies 79
12. A Double Blessing... 84
13. Someone is Watching You 90
14. Redeeming Your Time 98
15. Sowing Beside All Waters 106
16. Here Comes the Bride.. 111
17. Priceless Treasures... 117
18. To Trinidad for One Soul....................................... 124
19. God Uses Just Ordinary People 132
20. Become a Person of Passion 140
21. Win Them, One by One 148
22. Religious, but Lost.. 155
23. The Urgency of Our Mission 160
24. The Heavenly Wedding 167
25. The Crown of Rejoicing 173

~ This book represents the sole desire of my heart—to take to Heaven as many souls as I can, and to hear my Heavenly Father say, "Well done, thou good and faithful servant..." Matthew 25:21 ~

INTRODUCTION TO THE PROFESSION OF SOUL WINNING

"The seeds we sow today determine the kind of fruit we'll reap tomorrow." RBC Ministries

You are never more like God than when you give of yourself to others. You are never more a part of God than when you share His salvation. Acts 1:8 tells us, "...you shall be witnesses unto Me..." This is why God has put us here. Christians are the seed of the Almighty God. Isaiah 3:10 makes it clear that "...we will eat the fruit of our words..." We need to realize that our words have enormous creative power—they are like seeds that take root and grow.

God's Word is a seed. It is alive and full of unseen life. Remember that a seed does nothing until it's planted. The seed of the Word of God is powerful and sometimes it takes time to produce a harvest. Sometimes it springs up and bears fruit immediately in a person's life, but usually the seed grows over a period of time. We need to understand that a seed will stop growing without proper nourishment. As we scatter the seed, let's remember to water it with persistent prayer.

God gives an astounding promise in 2 Corinthians 9:10 where it says that the more seeds you sow, the more God will increase your supply of seed. He does this so you can be an even greater blessing to others.

When you scatter the seeds of eternal life to a lost and dying world, Jeremiah 1:12 tells us that He watches over His Word. "...I will hasten my word to perform it." The seeds of His Word that you sow will produce a harvest that He allows you to share in. Isn't it thrilling to know that God watches over those seeds you have sown to produce an abundant harvest of souls?

Have you ever had a conversation about spiritual things come up while you're at work or over lunch, and you felt a tug in your heart that just wouldn't go away? That tugging is the person of the Holy Spirit giving us an opportunity to share His eternal gift of salvation. Maybe you were tongue-tied and let the opportunity slide by. But if you keep praying for boldness and plead for soul winning power, God will set in your path hungry people to whom your witness is like manna from Heaven.

You do not know what wonderful opportunities God may have on your calendar. But there is a catch to being able to recognize these. Christians need to be so sensitive to the leading of the Holy Spirit in their lives that they know it was only God that brought that person into their path.

Do you desire to be a sweet fragrance to your Heavenly Father? When you are living your life to please Him, it's a beautiful aroma that attracts His attention. "For we are unto God a sweet savor of Christ..." (2 Corinthians 2: 15).

The sweet Psalmist of Israel tells us "To delight thyself in the Lord." Asking God for souls brings Him only delight, and this pleasant privilege of delighting ourselves in the Lord has a bountiful promise attached to it: "He shall give thee the desires of thine heart" (Psalm 37:4).

"Delight" in the Hebrew means to be "pliable." Are you allowing the Holy Spirit to mold your heart and shape your character so you can be used of God? When you and I make God's Word a priority in our lives, then, we are delighting in Him.

Do you realize that you can cause excitement in Heaven? Luke 15:10 tells us that we have the blessed privilege of augmenting the joy in Heaven. "Likewise, I say unto you, there is joy in the presence of the angels of God over one sinner that repenteth." Multitudes of angels are watching us, and express interest and joy when just one person turns to Christ. What soul winners we should prayerfully attempt to be! If the winning of just one soul to Jesus means such joy to the angels, what joy must flood the heart of our blessed Lord!

As a true believer in Jesus, the greatest treasure within you is the person of the Holy Spirit. I urge you to step into the future and make yourself available to Him. In this book you'll see that availability is one of the main keys to successful soul winning.

Have you ever wondered why some people win more souls than others? Is it because they have more opportunities? No. It's because they are available to God in every situation of their lives. Warren Wiersbe writes, "When God calls you to do a task for Him, He does not ask you to be adequate, He only asks you to be available."

Listen to wisdom! God tells us in Proverbs 2:4 to *search for it as you would for silver...Hunt for it like hidden treasure...and then you will begin to know God.* Solomon wrote in Proverbs 11:30 "...he that winneth souls is wise."

Daniel 12:3 assures us, "And they that be wise shall shine as the brightness of the firmament; and they that turn many to righteousness as the stars for ever and ever." Stars shine brilliantly like diamonds in the dark sky. God says that it is this wisdom that causes the soul winner to shine as brightly as those beautiful stars.

Many people dream of becoming a Hollywood star that the world praises and worships, but keep this thought it mind: Their stardom will not stand the test of time. Their names will soon be forgotten and their works will be nothing but ashes. God says that the faithful soul winner will outshine all these Hollywood celebrities for all eternity.

"He is wise who selects for his raw material immortal souls, whose existence shall outlast the stars. If God shall bless us to the winning of souls, our work shall remain when the wood, and hay, and stubble of earth's art and science shall have gone to the dust from which they sprang. In Heaven itself, the soul winner, blessed of God, shall have memorials of his work preserved forever in the galleries of the skies. He has selected a wise object, for what can be wiser than to glorify God; to snatch a soul from the gulf that yawns, to lift it up to the heaven that glorifies; to deliver an immortal from the thralldom of Satan, and to bring him into the liberty of Christ? What more excellent than this?"[1]

Catch a glimpse with me of a huge gathering—in eternity. God gives us a picture in Revelation 7:9 of millions of redeemed people around the throne of God. "... A great multitude, which no man can number, of all nations, and kindreds, and people, and tongues, stood before the throne and before the Lamb..." Do you see any of the world's wealth around the throne of God? We tend to focus on the here and now—our careers, bank accounts, education, beautiful homes and cars. While these things are important, they're only secondary to what really matters. Let me ask you, what part of that heavenly throng will be there because of you?

Christians all around the world were so inspired by the lives of five young missionary men that went to Ecuador to evangelize the isolated tribe of the Waodani Indians. They were totally focused on obedience to God's command no matter what the cost. In their mind's eye, they had a vision of Revelation 7:9 — precious Auca Indians standing before the Throne of God at the final roll-call. One of these missionaries, Jim Elliot, became an example of his own words: "He is no fool who gives up what he cannot keep to gain what he cannot lose."

We need to lift our eyes away from worldly things and focus our hearts on things that are eternal. Remember, we are in the world, but not of the world. He is calling us to see what He sees, and to share His heart for the harvest that will soon be gone if it is not reaped soon.

As you begin to read through this book, I challenge you to take a look at how you are investing your life. How much time do you spend in laboring for the riches of this world as compared to piling up riches for eternity?

You have only one life and God gives you the choice of how you will live it. Will you spend it on selfish desires and pleasures, or will you live your life for God's glory, knowing that He has promised eternal rewards? Once we have this treasure of eternal life within ourselves, God expects us to share this wonderful treasure with a lost world. We must not keep it to ourselves.

I have found that when you live your life in the light of eternity, earthly treasures that were once valuable become worthless. The only things we can take to Heaven are souls— souls that are precious in God's sight.

Close your eyes for a moment and imagine yourself in Heaven. All around you are people that you led to Christ. Or, maybe you were an indirect soul winner by giving to foreign missions. With tears of joy, they embrace you and thank you for giving them the Good News of salvation. Can there be any greater joy than this apart from the joy of seeing Jesus?

Please take a journey with me into an Indian Reservation, a hospital room in the Virgin Islands, a neighbor's house at 2:00 A.M., inside a prison cell, inside a home in Trinidad; these are just a few of the golden opportunities that the Lord has given me to share the good news of the gospel.

Remember, those who lay up treasures in Heaven are the richest people on earth!

Chapter 1

FIRST HAND EXPERIENCE

"The necessary qualification and prime importance of a witness is first-hand experience." J. Sidlow Baxter

Witnessing has to do with what we ourselves have proved and experienced in our own lives. One of the best tools that we can use in witnessing is our own personal testimony of God's work of grace in our lives. When a person is truly born again by the Spirit of God, He brings changes in our lives, and it is these changes that may encourage our unsaved friends and relatives to come to Christ for salvation.

There is a sphere that God operates in, and we cannot be a part of it until we acknowledge our sins and accept Jesus into our lives. Jesus makes it very plain in John 10:9 that He is the only way to Heaven. "I am the door: if any man enter in, he shall be saved, and shall go in and out, and find pasture." We cannot begin to understand the reality of spiritual things until we walk through that door and experience the mercy and grace of the Lord Jesus.

Let me give you my testimony. I was a child of nine when the Holy Spirit convicted me of my sins and I saw my need of a Savior. I put my trust in the precious blood of Jesus that day to save me and accepted Him as my Lord and Savior.

God convicts the sinner not only of "fleshly" sins as lying, stealing, murder, etc., but "...Of sin, because they believe not on me;" (John 16:9). The only sin that damns the soul is rejecting Jesus as your personal Savior.

When I asked Christ to be my personal Savior, I obtained that precious faith that the Apostle Peter wrote about in 2 Peter 1:2. "Grace and peace be multiplied unto you through the knowledge of God, and of Jesus our Lord." This verse speaks to us first of having a knowledge of Jesus. In the Greek, the word "knowledge" in this verse means a "personal knowledge."

God gave me a faith that was rooted in the knowledge of our Savior, and because of that, I can say with all assurance that I have a "knowing faith." There is an old saying that says, "The Blood makes me safe; the Word makes me sure." How true this is!

I Corinthians 1:3, tells us, "Grace be unto you, and peace, from God our Father, and from the Lord Jesus Christ." Grace is how we're saved, and it always comes first because we can't have the peace of God until we experience the wondrous grace of God through Jesus. Joy and peace are by-products of our salvation, and as we grow in our spiritual life, they become more of a reality in our lives. These are treasures that will outlive the grave and outshine the sun.

We not only should have "a knowing faith" but we should have "a growing faith," and that growing is our responsibility. 2 Peter 1:5 speaks of a different kind of knowledge than verse 2, "And beside this, giving all diligence, add to your faith virtue; and to virtue knowledge." Here, Peter tells of a "practical knowledge." A Christian is like a tree; if growth does not occur, decay sets in. And that's what will happen to our spiritual life.

We need to realize that when God saves us, He imparts to us His divine nature. Look at what the Apostle Peter says in 2 Peter 1:4: "Whereby are given unto us exceeding great and precious promises: that by these ye might be partakers of the divine nature..."

Do you realize that our behavior is determined by our nature? For example, it's the nature of fish to swim and birds to fly. If we truly have God's nature, then, we'll outwardly display that divine nature in various ways.

It's only natural that our new nature desires intimate fellowship with our Heavenly Father and also fellowship with other believers. If we don't have these desires, then we need to examine our hearts to see if we're really in the faith. "Examine yourselves, whether ye be in the faith; prove your own selves" (2 Corinthians 13:5).

We need to have a sense of certainty about our salvation before we can lead others to a saving knowledge of Christ. We can preach, teach or be a leader in a church, but we cannot be His witnesses until we experience that saving power in our lives. The following story illustrates this truth.

"That prince of the pulpit, the late J. H. Jowett, tells how his gifted preacher-friend, Dr. Charles Berry, first came into a saving experience of Christ after being in the ministry for years without really knowing Him as Savior."

"Late one night a Lancashire girl with a shawl over her head, and clogs on her feet, called at Dr. Berry's home. 'Are you a minister?' she asked. 'Then I want you to come and get my mother in.' Thinking she was referring to some drunken brawl, Dr. Berry said, 'You had better call a policeman to get your mother in.' 'No, no, sir; my mother is dying, and I want to get her into salvation.'

"Dr. Berry then enquired where she lived, and suggested that there might be another minister who lived nearer; but it was no use; she clung on determinedly. He wondered what the members of his fashionable church would say if they should see their minister out late at night with a girl of her appearance; but he just had to go."

"The house where she took him was one of ill fame. In the lower rooms they were drinking and indulging in lewd conversation, but upstairs was the poor dying woman. Dr. Berry sat down and knew he must somehow talk about Jesus; so he told about His beautiful life and teachings, until, with an awful look in her deathly eyes, the dying woman interrupted, 'Mister, that's no good for the likes o' me. I'm a sinner.'

"Dr. Berry was dumbstruck, suddenly realizing that he had no message for that poor, dying sinner. Then he recalled what his mother had taught him years before; and he began to tell the old, old story of God's love in Christ who died to be the Savior of sinners."

"Soon the dying woman spoke again: 'Now you're getting at it. That's what I want.' In relating the incident afterward, Dr. Berry added, 'And so I got her in—and at the same time I got in myself.'"[2]

I love the verse in John 12:32, where it says, "And I, if I be lifted up from the earth, will draw all men unto Me." It is not Christ apart from the cross who draws and saves. What unsaved people need to hear is not just a beautiful picture of the teachings of Christ—they need a cure for their sin. It is by pointing them to the Christ of Calvary where they see themselves as guilty sinners in need of a Savior.

Chapter 2

OUR FIRST PRIORITY

"Divine revelation is one of the greatest of divine favours, for God restores us to Himself by revealing Himself to us, and gives us all good by giving us knowledge."
Matthew Henry

If we belong to the Lord Jesus, what should be the deepest desire of our hearts? Is it not to please Him and serve Him? Our Lord asks us in the book of John, "Lovest thou Me?" Everything hinges on what our response will be. Our love for the Lord determines to what degree we will serve Him.

John Calvin was one of the greatest theologians who ever lived. He said, "I gave up all for Christ and what have I found? I have found everything in Christ." Do you honestly wish you could say that too? You can. Being a disciple of Christ means having fellowship with the Lord Jesus Christ. Always remember that fellowship with Christ always comes before service for Him. We must let Jesus minister to our needy hearts before we can minister effectively to others.

So many people say they love God, but rarely do they show it. We need to ask ourselves, "What do we love more than Jesus?" A true love for God cannot be kept inside without being shown on the outside—it'll eventually be manifested in the way a person thinks, talks, acts, and lives their life.

The first thing that makes a true disciple is not speaking ability, not how many degrees a person has behind his name, not even a love for souls, but a love-passion for Jesus Himself. If we serve Him without a heart of love and devotion, then our work will have been in vain. He wants love to be the driving factor behind everything we do. Listen to our Lord's parting words in John 14:21, "...he it is that loveth me: and he that loveth me shall be loved of my Father; and I will love him, and will manifest myself to him."

Because of His great love to us, He wants to draw us very near to Himself so we can bask in His presence. We live in a merciless, non-stop whirl of society, and we tend to forget those important things that would enrich our lives. God wants every day to call us away from the clamor of this world and feed our starved souls the Bread of Life. Do you realize that the greatest pleasure we can experience in this life is walking hand in hand with our Heavenly Father?

Psalm 34:8 implores us to prove the Lord to be true, "O taste and see that the Lord is good..." God is always waiting and ready to turn His heart toward the voice of His child. To think that Almighty God wants to talk with me, to hear my voice, and listen to my deepest longings is an amazing thing to me.

"Inspirato" is a Latin word that means "God breathes His words divinely into our souls." How incredible is His love for us as it leads us to experience the deep treasures of His Word. One of the reasons God wants us to be alone with Him is not just to benefit us, but also to share with others the gems He reveals to us. Do you realize that God blesses you so you can be a blessing to others? The Christian life is not meant to be hoarded; it is meant to be shared.

God can only manifest Himself to those believers who love Him enough to linger in His presence though the meditation of His Word and prayer. We'll never know the heart of Jesus by casual Bible reading and hurried prayer. Oh, we need to really seek Him with all our hearts.

He is the only One in whom are hid all those imperishable treasures that our souls crave so much. Listen to David in Psalm 119:2, "Blessed are they who keep his testimonies, and that seek him with the whole heart." Do you have a heart that earnestly craves the Lord Jesus? Just like this verse says, God gives you a promise of a happy and blessed life contingent on you craving God and obeying His commands.

"You're acquainted with physical thirst. Stop drinking and see what happens. Coherent thoughts vanish, skin grows clammy, and vital organs shut down. Deprive your body of necessary fluid, and it will tell you.

Deprive your soul of spiritual water, and it will tell you. Dehydrated hearts send desperate messages. Snarling tempers. Waves of worry. Growing guilt and fear. Hopelessness. Resentment. Loneliness. Insecurity.

But you don't have to live with a dehydrated heart. God invites you to treat your thirsty soul as you would treat your physical thirst. Just visit the WELL and drink deeply."[3]

How often we deny ourselves the experience of knowing Christ intimately, and because of this, we are in reality denying ourselves a foretaste of Heaven that God wants to give us so badly. We need to realize that God designed each of us to derive joy and happiness from being in His presence. This is why Solomon could write this precious verse in Song of Solomon 2:3, "...I sat down under his shadow with great delight, and his fruit was sweet to my taste."

Solomon felt the sweetness of communing with God. Oh, how we need to continually feed on Him and let our hearts really go out to Him. And, it is so true, that when we truly seek, we shall truly find. Only the one who truly loves the Lord will experience those rapturous moments of silent communion.

Some people like to put Jesus in a beautiful glass case or put Him in a picture frame with all the others we admire. But we cannot do that with our Lord because He can't be locked up in a frame—He walks right out of the past into the present, and desires to be our daily companion in every thing we do. But we so often push Him aside for our worldly pursuits. To really know Him should be the controlling desire of every believer.

But, let me add that if we so desire Him with all our hearts, then, there is a price to pay. Every day we need to give top priority to secret lingering in His presence, which can mean saying 'no' to fleshly desires that so war against our soul. It might mean losing an hour of sleep or turning off a favorite television show.

We need to make a godly determination to honor the Lord in every area of our lives. Our own family members and friends may not understand our devout devotion to the Lord, but always remember that living a life of consistent obedience will inspire others to do the same.

How can we tell if a person truly loves the Lord? I've jotted down four things that will be a priority in that person's life:

- There will be a deep craving for a personal communion with the Lord. King David describes it this way in Psalm 42:1, "As the hart panteth after the water brooks, so panteth my soul after thee, O God."

- There will be a passion for the souls of men. We won't be able to come into His presence in prayer without seeing the faces of the lost.

- There will be a longing for the return of Jesus—"Looking for that blessed hope, and the glorious appearing of the great God and our Savior Jesus Christ;" (Titus 2:13).

- There will be a love for other Christians and a real desire to fellowship with them. "We know that we have passed from death unto life, because we love the brethren. He that loveth not his brother abideth in death" (1 John 3:14).

The greatest privilege in the entire world is knowing Jesus as our Lord and Savior. As we grow in the knowledge of Christ, the more we should realize that our first priority in service to Him is soul winning. Christians should always be in the process of building bridges to unsaved people, and we do this by sharing our testimony of how the Lord saved us.

Many believers believe that service to our Lord is just sitting in church, teaching, church secretarial work, or committee work, etc. There's nothing wrong with these activities. We should be involved in church work, but they are only secondary to what we really should be doing—winning souls to the Savior.

Satan loves it when he sees us busy in the church, but the evil old Pharaoh hates the soul winner, and will do everything in his power to keep us from doing the most important work. Charles Spurgeon said it all with this statement: "Have you no wish for others to be saved? Then you are not saved yourself, be sure of that."

I like the words of Billy Sunday, "Every individual Christian a soul winner, and every local church an evangelizing center." And how far have we come from those words of wisdom!

Soul winning is a threefold challenge: First, it's the greatest service we can do for our fellow man. Second, it obeys the last of our Lord's commands. Third, the winning of souls receives the highest of all rewards in Heaven.

Chapter 3

"FOLLOW ME"

When we obey the Lord by following Him, He gives us a guarantee—He'll make us to become "fishers of men." This promise is contingent on our obedience.

The Washington Memorial is one of the tallest buildings in Washington, D.C., and it stands as a testimony to the great impact George Washington had on our nation. Written along the inside are quotes from Washington and words of wisdom from our first President. But one quotation on the Washington Memorial isn't as widely noted. During the 1990's, the memorial was remodeled, and while being remodeled, workers found some "graffiti" etched into the memorial. One phrase that was of particular interest was this: *Whoever is the human instrument under God in the conversion of one soul, erects a monument to his own memory more lofty and enduring than this.* That phrase was uncovered and preserved so that visitors today can view it.

It makes me proud to know that some of our founding fathers were not just great leaders, but some were avid followers of God and great soul winners. Whoever etched this wise saying is conveying to us the concept that being a soul winner for Christ has a far greater impact than any monument of great men.

Do you realize that everyone follows something in life, whether it is a person, thing, or a hobby? The decision we must face isn't whether or not to follow, but what we will follow. Our Heavenly Father desires that we would choose to follow Him above anything else in our lives.

When we make the choice to follow the Lord, we have to realize that He wants total surrender of our wills, our minds, and our bodies. But I must also warn you that if you do make this decision to follow, then know that you have chosen to walk a narrow path. It involves a cost—there will be inconveniences, difficulties, pain and counterattacks from Satan. Our only concern is to belong to Him and have His approval stamped upon our lives.

What does the word, "follow" mean? I once read of a missionary that was trying to explain this word to the native people. She used the illustration of walking—we are "to follow right on one's heels." It is the word for following closely, not at a distance. We are to follow Jesus as closely as we can.

In Matthew 4:19, Jesus is giving His disciples a command, "...Follow me, and I will make you fishers of men." Jesus did not teach his disciples in a classroom setting; He taught them through example. First, they had to observe and follow Jesus before they could be workers for Him. He desired that they would be more than spectators of the gospel—He longed for them to be followers and participants.

Now, fast forward to the end of Matthew to chapter 28:19, 20 where before His ascension, Jesus gave His disciples a last pep talk: "Go ye therefore, and teach all nations, baptizing them in the name of the Father, and of the Son, and of the Holy Ghost: Teaching them to observe all things whatsoever I have commanded you: and, lo, I am with you always, even unto the end of the world." And every one of them eventually laid down their lives for preaching the gospel.

The disciples had observed and learned from the Lord. Now, it was time to step out into the world and participate in ministry without Jesus' physical presence. John 14:12 confirms that He totally believed in them. "Verily, verily, I say unto you, He that believeth on me, the works that I do, he shall do also; and greater works than these shall he do; because I go unto my Father."

Did you notice something in that verse? Jesus wasn't just talking to His disciples—He was also addressing you and me. Jesus believes in you! Jesus' ministry was cut off when He was about thirty-three years old. Since then, great soul winners, such as Billy Sunday, Charles Spurgeon, George Whitefield, Dr. John R. Rice, and others have preached to more people and won more souls than were saved by the personal ministry of Jesus.

The call to discipleship is a call to soul winning. I think so many times we do not realize what our part consists of in carrying out the Great Commission. There are not any of us that can save a soul or put anyone under conviction. The Holy Spirit is the one doing the soul winning. We are only the human tools that God chooses to use in sowing the seed. It is not our job to save anyone—it is to follow in the footsteps of our Lord, and do it as He did, and then, stand back and watch God work.

Just like the fisherman, we can't make the fish take the bait on the hook—our part is to put the bait out there, and we can do this in several ways:

- By having a burden for lost people, and in turn that burden will cause us to pray for their salvation.

- By letting our lights shine—Our testimony should be salty. As the "salt of the earth," Christians can make others thirsty for the water of life.

- By spreading the gospel on the home front and in foreign lands. Acts 1:8 tells us to do this both at the same time. "...And ye shall be witnesses unto me both in Jerusalem, and in all Judea, and in Samaria, and unto the uttermost part of the earth."

- By letting others see the joy of the Lord in our lives. "Rejoice in the Lord always, and again, I say, Rejoice" (Philippians 4:4).

Does the soul winner always get instant results when witnessing? No. In some people's lives, evangelism is a process that may take years—it may take a long time for God to move these people to saving faith. Then, there are others that are "ripe for harvest" and are ready to be saved the first time they hear the message of salvation.

Fishermen know that different kinds of bait are required to catch different types of fish. In the same way, as we share the gospel, we may use various approaches, depending on the person's situation. Of course, Jesus, is our example. He never dealt with any two people in exactly the same way.

If we were talking to a dying person, we would address the subject of eternity and the certainty of Heaven for those who put their trust in Christ. If we're witnessing to someone who is filled with fear and anxiety, we might speak to them of the peace that only God can give. Another person might be plagued with past guilt, so we might speak to them about God's complete forgiveness.

It is true that not everyone will get saved, but some will. But if we do our part in simply following Jesus, then, God will do His. Philip with the Ethiopian Eunuch and Andrew with his brother, Simon, are just a few of the examples throughout the New Testament of this principle.

Picture the following scene in Heaven after Jesus ascended 2000 years ago, and just suppose the following conversation took place between Jesus and the angel, Gabriel. Keep in mind that God doesn't have a plan A, a plan B and a plan C for evangelizing the world. He has only one plan and that plan is you and me.

"Gabriel: "Master, you died for the whole world down there, did you not?"

Jesus: "Yes."

Gabriel: "You must have suffered much."
(with an earnest look into the wonderful but scarred face).

Jesus: "Yes."

Gabriel: "And do they all know about it?"

Jesus: "Oh, no: only a few people in Palestine know about it, so far."

Gabriel: "Well, Master, what is your plan? What has been done about telling the world that you have died and provided redemption?"

Jesus: "I asked Peter, James, and John, and Andrew, and some others of them down there, to make it the business of their lives to tell others; and the others are to tell others, and the others still others, until the last man in the farthest circle has heard."

Gabriel: (Who feels doubt about the plan after contacts with us folk down here) "Yes, but suppose Peter fails?... Suppose that after a time John fails?...and suppose they do not tell others? Or suppose that those who come afterward fail to keep on telling others...What then?"

Jesus: (With eyes full of tenderness and longing) "Gabriel, I haven't made any other plan. I'm counting on them."[4]

Chapter 4

OBJECTIONS TO THE GOSPEL

"If the Bible is truly God's Word to us, and if we reject its message of salvation, then no other personal decision we make will be more consequential." John Ankerberg

Whenever we try to lead people to the Lord, we'll invariably hear objections and reasons why they don't want to be saved. In this chapter I'll just name a few.

As Christians, we will all face times when we need God's wisdom. Whether it is counseling a friend, witnessing to a lost person, or responding to a critic, we must have God's wisdom. Responding before seeking God will usually lead to misspoken words. You've heard the old saying, "Think before you speak," but a wiser saying would be, "Pray before you speak."

Just suppose that you were among a group of people that were mocking Christianity and the resurrection of Jesus. Would you remain silent or would you respond and if so, what would you say?

I Peter 3:15 instructs the believer to be always ready to defend the faith. "Be ready always to give an answer to every man that asketh you a reason of the hope that is in you with meekness and fear." Peter is saying that Christians need to be grounded in the Word of God so they'll always have a ready answer. We need to be able to answer the questions of an unbeliever without a second thought.

Making sure you know what you believe will require diligent work on your part. Dig into the Scriptures and don't be afraid to seek guidance from godly people. This is so important as the lost person you're trying to share your faith with wants to know what you believe and why.

When you stand for the truth, you will be open to mockery and ridicule, but you'll be in good company. The ungodly laughed Jesus to scorn on several occasions. Keep in mind what people need is the truth of Christ, because He is the only solid-rock foundation in this world. All other foundations are built on sinking sand.

Remember, too, that we need to pray that God will open their eyes to the truth. Satan is in the business of blinding the eyes of the unsaved so that they remain in darkness. This is why we have people that are resistant to our witness. But, on the other hand, Jesus is in the business of restoring sight to the blinded eyes. "I am the light of the world; he that followeth me shall not walk in darkness, but shall have the light of life" (John 8:12).

"I BELIEVE IN GOD, ISN'T THAT ENOUGH?"

What people don't realize is that just a general belief in God will not save them. Neither, according to the Word of God, can our church membership, baptism, nor confirmation attain for us eternal life.

I always quote James 2:19 to these people. "Thou believest that there is one God; thou doest well; the devils also believe, and tremble." Satan and his demons (fallen angels) have an intellectual belief in God and are aware of His awesome power. The demons, unlike man, tremble or shudder, and are terrified at the thought of God.

This verse in James helps us understand that saving faith is not the intellectual acceptance of the fact that "God is." The faith that saves is one that not only believes that God is, but also changes a person's life. That's saving faith. If we believe only that God is, that puts us only on the same level as the demons. They believe in fear, but they will not obey God.

I always stress that salvation is a personal matter between God and man. The one and true God is not like the false gods of this world—God, in the person of the Lord Jesus, wants a personal relationship with us; and we only obtain this by repenting of our sins and trusting Jesus as our own personal Savior. "True conversion is God, immediately known and possessed in the heart through direct invasion by the Holy Spirit." J. Sidlow Baxter.

"I HAVE PLENTY OF TIME. I WANT TO HAVE FUN. I'LL BECOME A CHRISTIAN LATER."

Knowing the danger of delay, I'll usually ask them this question: "If you were to die right now, where would you go?" If he realizes that he would go to Hell, he may not resist much longer.

I don't think you would find one person in Hell who deliberately planned to go there, but each waited too late and died without the Savior. In the book of Acts, Paul talked with Felix about his soul, and Felix answered back by saying, "Go thy way for this time; when I have a convenient season, I will call for thee."

The Bible does not say if Felix ever called for Paul. If Felix never accepted Christ, then he is suffering the torments of Hell, not because he wanted to go there, but because he waited for a "convenient season."

I believe that Hell has enlarged itself because of people that have waited to be saved at a later date, but death came suddenly and they weren't ready.

The following tragic story is from a sermon by Pastor Curtis Hutson—may it speak to your heart as it did mine:

"In this congregation sits a young man that I led to Christ. He was so burdened about his brother, in his twenties, that he took off from work and went to Florida to try to lead him to Christ. He said to his brother, 'I'm saved, and I want you to be saved. I want to tell you how to get saved.' They prayed. As he tried to show his brother how to get saved, his brother laughed at him! 'I'm young. I have plenty of time to get saved later on. Leave me alone! I am just in my twenties.'

This man came back to Atlanta brokenhearted because his brother wouldn't accept Christ. A week later his brother picked up a hitchhiker. The hitchhiker picked up a revolver and unloaded six shots into him and dumped him out in the desert in Florida. He was found a few weeks later and brought back here. I conducted his funeral. When I stood over that casket, I could almost hear him say, 'Leave me alone. I'm young. I have plenty of time to get saved later on.'"

"THERE ARE TOO MANY HYPOCRITES IN THE CHURCH."

One of the biggest complaints against the church is that it's full of hypocrites. Unfortunately, it's true. Too many people that sit in the pews live like unbelievers. The unbeliever can live the same way and sleep on Sunday. We, as true believers, need to desperately practice what we preach.

Hypocrites are in every profession of life—you don't quit going to physicians because some are quacks —you don't throw away money because there's counterfeit money. Remember that one of the twelve disciples, Judas, was a hypocrite. I love what Dr. Adrian Rogers says regarding this, "It's the counterfeit that proves the validity of the real."

Don't let a hypocrite keep you away from Jesus. Personally, I'd rather spend my life in church with a few hypocrites than spend eternity in Hell with all of them.

"HOW DO YOU KNOW THE BIBLE IS THE WORD OF GOD?"

Keep in mind that even though we know the Bible is 100-percent true; we can't force people to believe it. And, no matter how much evidence we give them, they still may not believe. We have to remember that the un-regenerate heart is wicked, and until the light of the gospel shines in their heart, they will not believe.

The Apostle Paul wrote in 2 Timothy 3:15, "All scripture is given by inspiration of God, and is profitable for doctrine, for reproof, for correction, for instruction in righteousness." The Bible can be trusted as the inspired, inerrant Word of God. Peter tells us in 2 Peter 1:21, "For the prophecy came not in old time by the will of man: but holy men of God spake as they were moved by the Holy Ghost."

The Bible is not just an ordinary book—It is the living, powerful Word of God (Hebrews 4:12), in which we encounter the Lord and discover how to live for Him and honor Him. I love what Dr. Adrian Rogers says about the Bible, "You read other books, but this Book reads you."

We know the Bible to be the true Word of God because of its scientific and historical accuracy. True science always agrees with the Bible. The book of Job tells us, "He stretcheth out the north over the empty place, and hangeth the earth upon nothing." And, Isaiah states, "It is he that sitteth upon the circle of the earth."

"Moses was the greatest scientist who ever lived. On every subject which he treats he is an authority, and not one of his instructions given in the Pentateuch on medicine, surgery, hygiene, astronomy, psychology or other branches has ever needed correction or revision." Dr. M. R. DeHaan, M.D.

For instance, in Leviticus 15, we read where Moses knew all about bacteriology, and he sets down Biblical rules for disinfection of contagious diseases. We also read in the books of Leviticus and Deuteronomy where he laid down the fundamental principles of agriculture and horticulture.

I would recommend studying the outstanding book, *The Chemistry of the Blood*, by the late Dr. M. R. DeHaan. In it, his scientific background is uniquely combined with his skillful exposition of Scripture, to correlate Scripture and science.

The truthfulness of the Bible is supported by a mountain of archeological evidence and centuries of fulfilled prophecies. There are over three hundred prophecies in the Old Testament about the first coming of the Messiah that were literally fulfilled without error in Jesus' life and ministry. We read in Psalm 22 and Isaiah 52 about specific details about death by crucifixion hundreds of years before this terrible form of execution was ever practiced.

Another example of fulfilled prophecy was the destruction of the city of Tyre. Hundreds of years before, Ezekiel predicted that the city would be destroyed and would never be rebuilt. It happened exactly as predicted, and today, it is a silent witness to the accuracy of Bible prophecy.

In the book of Daniel, four great world powers were predicted: Babylon, Medo-Persia, Greece, and Rome. It all came to pass. The predictions of the judgment of God against Nineveh, Ammon and Moab, Babylon, and Edom were all fulfilled as prophesied.

Just as His first coming was fulfilled, we know that the second coming of Jesus will be fulfilled as well. Prophetic signposts clearly indicate we are fast approaching the final midnight hour when Christ will return. We look forward to His coming with great anticipation, "Looking for the blessed hope, and the glorious appearing of the great God and our Savior Jesus Christ" (Titus 2:13).

The discovery of the Dead Sea Scrolls in 1947 has been called the greatest archaeological discovery of the 20th century. The ancient manuscripts are the oldest known copies of key Old Testament books. With every discovery made by the spade of archaeology, it speaks to a skeptical and disbelieving world.

"Modern criticism of the Bible began in the late 1700's and has continued to this day. The usual claim, often from Bible scholars, has been that the Bible is nothing more than error-filled writings.

"Before serious excavation work had begun in the mid-1800's, scholars felt free to consider lack of evidence as proof that people, cities, and even whole nations mentioned in the Bible never existed. It didn't seem to matter to them that they had never even bothered to look for evidences. And, with each discovery, the critics' pronouncements about errors in the Bible began to crumble.

"Every claim that there is error in the Bible has been based upon lack of knowledge. Let's face it, no matter what the subject, including history; God has more knowledge than we do."[5]

Pride fills the hearts of intellectual skeptics. We have to remember that they have been given a lot of misinformation and are confused with worldly wisdom. They do not possess pure wisdom that only comes from God. They do not understand that the beginning of wisdom begins with acceptance of Jesus as Savior and Lord. I have noticed that these kinds of people do not lead very happy lives. How can they? They don't have the joy of the Lord in their lives.

The way to win these people is to very patiently love them and fervently pray for Holy Spirit conviction that will lead them to a saving knowledge of Christ.

"WILL I HAVE TO GIVE UP MY DRINKING?"

Another common question is, "Will I have to give up my live-in relationship?" When I'm asked questions like this, I always say, "Yes." And let me tell you why. It's because they're already convicted of these sins—or else they wouldn't bring up the subject.

With this kind of person, I quote Matthew 9:13, 14 "Enter ye in at the strait gate: for wide is the gate, and broad is the way, that leadeth to destruction, and many there be which go in thereat: Because strait is the gate, and narrow is the way, which leadeth unto life, and few there be that find it."

Many people have believed a watered-down gospel that deletes the message of repentance. This is a false gospel and not the biblical faith that leads to eternal life.

"I JUST CANNOT BELIEVE THAT THERE IS AN ACTUAL HELL."

Actually, Jesus talks more about a place called Hell then He does about Heaven. Hell is a literal, awful, eternal reality. And people will be there because they rejected Christ in this life. We have to realize that separation from God is eternal—there is no parole from Hell and there is no purgatory.

Jesus draws back the curtain in Luke 16:22 to give us a glimpse of this horrible place. "The rich man also died, and was buried; And in Hell he lift up his eyes, being in torments." Hell is not a state of the mind, but a real place, just like Heaven is a real place. "For their worm shall not die, neither shall their fire be quenched" (Isaiah 66:24). The rich man was not annihilated or unconscious in this story. This should bring tears to our eyes and a godly fear to our hearts as we not only make sure of our own destiny, but also of the eternal state of others.

Jesus continually warned men to stay out of this terrible place. Revelation 20 sheds more light on Hell, or the lake of fire. Hell was originally created for Satan and his evil angels, but Isaiah 5:14 informs us that "Hell hath enlarged herself," because there have been so many people that have rejected the Lord Jesus. God does not send people to Hell; they send themselves there by their unbelief.

But there is good news—nobody has to go there. On the flip side of the coin there is a beautiful place called Heaven. John 14:2, 3 tells us, "In my Father's house are many mansions....I go to prepare a place for you. And if I go and prepare a place for you, I will come again, and receive you unto myself; that where I am, there ye may be also."

"I DON'T THINK I'M A SINNER, I CONSIDER MYSELF A PRETTY GOOD PERSON."

Imagine thinking that you are headed for Heaven, but you discover when you get to the gate of eternity that the ticket you have is worthless. It can happen when we trust in ourselves to take us there. When someone tells me that they're not a sinner, I quote Romans 3:23, "For all have sinned and come short of the glory of God." I John 1:8 tells us, "If we say that we have no sin, we deceive ourselves, and the truth is not in us."

I have heard so many people say, "I'm sure I'll be going to Heaven because I'm a pretty good person." And, I ask them, "How good is good enough?" You would never know if you've done enough to satisfy a Holy God. Besides, God demands absolute perfection. Being a good person is commendable, but our goodness cannot save us, because we can never measure up to God's standards.

Before we become a child of God, Isaiah 64:6 tells us, "All our righteousnesses are as filthy rags." Another verse is found in Titus 3:5. "Not by works of righteousness which we have done, but according to his mercy he saved us by the washing of regeneration, and renewing of the Holy Ghost." Mercy and grace are key words in salvation—they mean "undeserved favor" that God extends to us sinful creatures. And He is rich in mercy, which means He has plenty of it.

God offers us a free ticket to Heaven, but only because the Lord Jesus has already paid the ultimate price for it. The road to salvation begins first with the acknowledgment of our sin before a Holy God, and putting our complete trust in His shed blood to wash away our sins. We can claim our ticket to Heaven by simply believing that God's way to Heaven is the only way.

"WHAT ABOUT THOSE WHO HAVE NEVER HEARD THE GOSPEL?"

Is God fair or just to let a person go to Hell without ever hearing the Name of Jesus? The Apostle Paul gives us such a clear answer to this in the first two chapters of Romans. Let me just summarize a sermon by Dr. Adrain Rogers on this subject.

First of all, there is the revelation factor. John 1:9 states very clearly, "That was the true Light, which lighteth every man that cometh into the world." All men are sinners, but all men are called of God and are to some degree enlightened. God has given mankind adequate knowledge so that every man is without excuse.

Let me paint a scenario of that future court day when all the unsaved will stand before Almighty God at the Great White Throne Judgment. God will open the books and each person will be asked, "What did you do with Jesus?" Many will cry out, "I never had a chance to hear the gospel, I'm not guilty." Then, two witnesses will be called to the stand as God shows us why they are guilty.

The first witness is *Creation*, which is the outward witness. Romans 1:20 tells us, "For the invisible things of him from the creation of the world are clearly seen, being understood by the things that are made, even his eternal power and Godhead; so that they are without excuse." Other Scriptures that shed more light on this are Psalm 98:2, 3 and Psalm 19:1-6.

The second witness is *Conscience,* which is the inward witness. Listen to Paul in Romans 2:15, "Which show the work of the law written in their hearts, their conscience also bearing witness, and their thoughts the mean while accusing or else excusing one another." Even if the unsaved do not have the written Law, they have the Law written on their hearts, pressed by their God-given conscience. Another word for conscience in the Bible is "Candle of the Lord" (Proverbs 20:27).

Then, there is the refusal factor found in Romans 1:21, 22, "Because that, when they knew God, they glorified him not as God, neither were thankful; but became vain in their imaginations, and their foolish heart was darkened. Professing themselves to be wise, they became fools." Though some have greater light and knowledge than others, yet all have enough to leave them inexcusable. If people do not glorify God with the light they have, they begin to regress, and they will lose what light they do have. Always remember that *Light refused increases darkness.*

"Ever since Adam and Eve listened to Satan, the lies have grown and have effectively buried the truth. And when the truth surfaces, people push it back down because they don't want God's light shining on their dark errors." Martin R. DeHaan II.

If people suppress the light that's already in their hearts, then God gives them over to a depraved mind. Romans 1:28 states, "And even as they did not like to retain God in their knowledge, God gave them over to a reprobate mind, to do those things which are not convenient." Romans 1:22-32 shows the result of a reprobate mind: Perverted religion, heathenism, idolatry, homosexuality, and depravity.

So how does God judge these people that choose darkness over the light? They will not be judged because they did not hear about Christ, but because they have rebelled against the knowledge they did have about God. From the very beginning of time mankind has had freedom of choice, and a responsibility to know and obey the truth. See Genesis 2:16, 17; 3:6, 7 and Romans 1:18-25. They will have no excuse when they stand before a Holy, Sovereign God.

Lastly, we have the receptive factor. *Light obeyed increases light.* God has given us enough knowledge in the universe to serve as a basis for seeking to know more about Him. The two witnesses shows we have a "built-in" knowledge of God. Paul illustrates this when he addressed the intellectuals in the city of Athens in Acts 17:16-34. Other examples of this are with the Ethiopian Eunuch in Acts 8:26-40 and with Cornelius seeking God in Acts 10. God will always give us more light if we honestly seek more light.

There are documented examples of remote heathen tribes in Asia that had been seeking the true God for some time but didn't know who He was. These groups spoke of a lost holy book and a broken relationship with the Creator. Because they obeyed the little light that they did have, they were overjoyed when God sent them missionaries so they could hear the truth of God's Word.

"What are you doing with the little light that God has so graciously placed within your heart?" It's a very dangerous thing to ignore that light and reject the gospel. God gives us a wonderful promise found in Jeremiah 29:13, "And ye shall seek me, and find me, when ye shall search for me with all your heart."

Chapter 5

AN ENTIRE FAMILY WON TO CHRIST

Heaven will be much sweeter if you see people there because you were that instrument God used to bring them to salvation.

Have you ever felt that God used you in an "indirect" way in soul winning? Well, let me tell you of an incident that happened to me in this particular way. As our church was having evangelistic meetings, I prayed that God would lead me to certain nurses at work that I could invite to these services. He answered my prayers, but not in the way I thought He would.

Perhaps you can remember a time when you were involved in a series of revival meetings. Was your heart stirred for the lost in your community? Were there nights where believers poured out their hearts to the Lord? I can remember such a time when the power of God was upon our meetings and souls were being saved.

At that particular time, I was attending a good soul winning church. I shall always be immensely grateful to my minister and wife, Warren and Joyce Webster, that took me under their wing and gave me spiritual guidance during a difficult time in my life. Joyce and I developed a beautiful friendship, and through her example I soon caught the vision of perishing souls. We became soul-winning partners, and what a blessed time of fellowship we had when we would knock on doors to give out the gospel message.

Pastor Warren and Joyce Webster

The week before the meetings started, I took a handful of church brochures to work with me, as I planned on giving them to certain nurses that the Lord had laid on my heart. I especially had a very heavy burden for a certain unsaved nurse that I had known for some time. As I was talking to her on our lunch break about these meetings, unbeknown to me, another nurse, Diana, had overheard us talking and later came to me and asked what church I attended.

I was overjoyed that Diana was interested in the meetings. She said, "My husband and I have a real desire to study the Bible. We've been looking for a good church, but we're confused as to which one to attend." So I gave her a brochure of the meetings and gave her a special invitation. I didn't know her too well, and I'll have to admit that I didn't have much faith that she would come. God is so good to us even when we have feelings of doubt.

Diana brought her teen-age daughter to church that week. The evangelist was preaching on *"How to raise your children,"* not really an evangelistic sermon, but the Lord used the message to bring conviction upon their hearts. At the invitation time, they both came forward for salvation, and Joyce had the blessed privilege of leading those two precious souls to the Lord. Oh, how that blessed my heart!

Two weeks later Diana's husband started coming to church. He didn't get saved at that time, but he listened intently to the Word of God as it was being preached. Some time later Pastor Webster went to visit him, and the Lord gave him the privilege of leading this dear man to the Lord. It was such a blessing to see this family grow spiritually and take an active part in the church.

Five years after they were saved, their daughter expressed interest in getting a good Bible education. She attended a fundamental Bible College, met a wonderful Christian man, and now her and her husband are serving the Lord. I had a chance to talk with them some time ago, and it blessed my heart to hear that they are still faithful in the Lord's work.

Sometimes things might not happen as we expect, but we should always expect the unexpected from our Lord. I was so intent on witnessing to my good friend that I wasn't even thinking of others, and the Lord gave me a nice surprise when this entire family was won to Christ.

A Biblical example of "indirect" soul winning would be supporting missionaries on a foreign field. The money we send to them enables them to give the glorious gospel to those who have never heard the name of Jesus. Keep in mind that indirect soul winning does not excuse us for what we should be doing on the home front. Acts 1:8 reminds us that we should be witnesses of Christ "...Both in Jerusalem, and in all Judea, and in Samaria, and unto the uttermost part of the earth." We are to be soul winners at home and abroad at the same time.

Does it pay to pray and witness for the Lord? Oh, yes, it does! There's no greater joy than seeing people trust the Lord for salvation, and then, to see them grow spiritually. We can't take credit for any of it. All praise and honor belongs to Jesus because it is He that gives the increase.

The Dutch evangelistic, Corrie ten Boom, had a God-given desire to win others to Christ. Let me quote from one of her poems that so blessed my heart:

"When I enter that beautiful city, and the saints all around me appear, I hope that someone will tell me, it was you who invited me here."

Wouldn't you, too, like the thrilling experience of seeing others become a part of God's family? You might begin by making a list of unbelieving family and friends. And, as you pray, God will give you a heartfelt burden for their salvation. This concern will likely make you more motivated to live a godly life in front of them, and God will give you opportunities to share the gospel with them.

"It pays to serve Jesus, it pays every day, It pays every step of the way; Though the pathway to Glory may sometimes be drear, You'll be happy each step of the way."
Frank C. Huston

Chapter 6

GET OUT OF YOUR COMFORT ZONE

Soul winning is the responsibility of every Christian, and the Bible praises those who will step out of their comfort zone and share the gospel with the lost around them.

Let me introduce to you a soul-winner in Acts 10. The Lord had instructed Simon Peter, a Jew, to go to the city of Caesarea and witness to Cornelius, a Gentile. Cornelius was a Roman centurion, and also a very religious, devout man that feared God and prayed continually to Him.

Even though he was a non-Jew, he kept calling out to their God. Because Cornelius was truly seeking God, He sent an angel to tell him to call for Peter, who would tell him the gospel story. I read in Jeremiah 29:13 that God will reveal Himself to the true seeker. "And ye shall seek me, and find me, when ye shall search for me with all your heart."

Before the Apostle Peter left for Caesarea, God gave him a vision—a vision that explained that the gospel includes all people, Jew and Gentile, the good and bad. Up until now, Peter had been preaching to the Jews only and had no desire to include the Gentiles.

Christ had given the command to teach all nations, but Peter had not fully understood this command until it was here revealed by a vision. Peter had to step out of his comfort zone and change his attitude toward the Gentiles before God could use him. Because he obeyed the Lord, Cornelius and all his family heard the gospel and were saved. Please note three important truths in this story that we can apply to our own lives:

- No matter how moral and religious we are, we cannot be saved without hearing the gospel. Cornelius was a very religious person, but was lost without Jesus in his life.

- Christians are God's instruments to reach the lost with the good news of salvation. Romans 10:14 tells us, "...how shall they hear without a preacher?"

- In some of our circumstances in life, are we willing to change some things for the sake of the gospel? Peter was a very prejudiced Jew until the Lord changed his heart.

Several years ago I took a job in Home Health where a few of my patients were Nez Perce Indians. I never will forget Joseph, an elderly Indian who was a very prominent leader of the tribe. During the months I took care of him, I got well acquainted with their traditional religion and practices. Knowing that their beliefs are well steeped in demonism, I became very burdened for him and his family and prayed that the Lord would use me in his salvation.

Many Nez Perce have adopted Christianity, but they combine it with beliefs of the Dreamer religion, which is a traditional Nez Perce faith. They believe that their former leaders were given special dreams and visions that predicted important events. And, they believe that present-day leaders receive spiritual power from their ancestors and the environment.

"A Great Power, sometimes called Great Spirit or Great Mystery underlies all creation. This power is not a personal god, such as the Judeo-Christian God, and it cannot be imagined in human form. Rather, it is a universal force to which all of nature is attuned.

Values, beliefs, morals, ethics, and sacred traditions are passed on through an oral tradition and through ceremonies. These commonly include dancing, singing, drumming, and feasting, as well as purification rites, fasting, and physical ordeals.

Certain people called medicine men or women have special ties to the higher powers. Their special calling enables them to mediate between the spirit world and the earthly world for healing, spiritual renewal, and the good of the community."[6]

As I began to witness to him he began to ask questions about my faith, and I could tell he was deeply concerned about what would happen to him after he died. He was bedridden at that time, and I knew he only had a short time to live.

I shared with him my testimony of how I came to know the Lord at an early age. After listening intently, he said, "I believe in the Christian God that you're telling me about, but I also believe in my traditional Indian religion." I replied, "Joseph, the Bible says that we cannot combine Jesus with any other religion." Then, I showed him John 14:6 where it plainly says that Jesus is the only way to Heaven.

I showed him Galatians 1:8 where it says that anyone that perverts the true gospel will be accursed. "But though we, or an angel from heaven, preach any other gospel unto you than that which we have preached unto you, let him be accursed." I continued by showing him Revelation 22:18 where it plainly says that we are not to add anything to what Jesus tells us in His Word. I said, "Joseph, if you're willing to forsake your Indian religion and turn to Jesus for salvation, then Jesus will cleanse your heart and save you."

I'll never forget the answer he gave me. He said, "Helen, I know the Bible is true, and now I know why I've never had any peace in my heart. In my younger days, while watching the various tribal dances, I would feel the presence of evil and I just knew in my heart that something wasn't right."

All his life Joseph had been taught that the god he worshipped could not be known in a personal way. As I read to him the chapters in John 3 and John 10, the light began to dawn upon him that Jesus wanted to be his personal Savior and Shepherd, and that he could not go to Heaven without a personal relationship with Him. As I gently showed him how to be saved, he told me with tears in his eyes that he didn't understand such wonderful love, but he believed and accepted it.

Joseph became a true believer in the Lord Jesus, and I know I'll see him in Heaven some day. He used to love to listen to passages of Scripture on Heaven, especially John 14:1-6, where it speaks of the hope that we have in Jesus and the blessed glory-land that awaits all believers. Jesus gave him a blessed hope that his Indian religion could not give him.

Always remember that the primary way that God reaches people is through people. The angel God sent to Cornelius could have very easily given him the gospel, but that's not God's way of reaching people. Peter was the man whom God wanted to use to reach Cornelius. God wanted Cornelius to be saved, and He also wanted to use the conversion of Cornelius, a Gentile, to open Peter's eyes to the fact that there is a big world out there that needs to hear the gospel.

In I Timothy 2:4 the Apostle Paul says, "Who will have all men to be saved, and to come unto the knowledge of the truth." "All men" include that neighbor, that co-worker, that grocery-clerk who has a different culture and background than us. There is no room for bigotry or prejudice, and no room for bias in the life of the Christian. The Bible says, *There is no respect of persons with God*, and every soul is precious in His sight. My prayer is that the Holy Spirit will give us the vision of the faces of people crying out for life that only the Lord Jesus can give.

Chapter 7

ARE YOU ADAPTABLE?

"Sometimes we don't understand the leading of God in our lives, but we have to remember that God's commands are sometimes contrary to human reasoning and can be unappealing to our natural minds." Author Unknown

The opportunities of the Holy Spirit are often unclear to us. This truth is demonstrated in the story of Philip and the Ethiopian eunuch in Acts 8:26-40. Philip was doing an extensive work for God in Samaria when He called him to leave what he was doing and go out into the desert land of Gaza. I find here a very interesting truth. Philip wasn't told why he should go; he heard the voice of God and immediately obeyed.

Philip probably wondered why God would call him from a big work to go off on a wild-goose chase down a lonely desert road. He could have easily argued with the Lord. He could have said, "What do you mean, 'Go to the desert?' I am having a fruitful ministry here in Samaria. Get someone else to go." Many Christians, like Philip, have found to obey the promptings of the Spirit will bring blessed results and far-reaching consequences.

On the desert road Philip encountered an Ethiopian eunuch who was traveling to Jerusalem to worship God. He was a very religious man, but was not a Christian. When Philip saw him, he was reading Isaiah 53, which is the clearest picture in the Old Testament of the coming of the Messiah. The eunuch invited Philip to sit with him in the chariot. Philip took advantage of this opportunity to tactfully ask him if he understood what he was reading.

You can readily see the frustration of the eunuch at being unable to understand this particular passage, and he told Philip he needed someone to guide him. I love verse 35, "Then Philip opened his mouth, and began at the same scripture, and preached unto him Jesus." And immediately the eunuch received Jesus as his own personal Savior.

I want you to notice something in verse 29 that really spoke to my heart. "Then the Spirit said unto Philip, Go near, and join thyself to this chariot." The chariot did not come to Philip; Philip ran to the chariot. Opportunities sometimes come into our lives for a brief time and we have to act fast or else it will pass us by. We need to go after lost people with the gospel and compel them to be saved. Does not the Great Commission tell us to "GO?" The Word of God cannot be any plainer that that.

Philip did not know that he was witnessing to a man that had great authority under the Queen of Ethiopia, and that the gospel would be sent to all of North Africa through this eunuch. Just think of the wonderful blessing that came from this encounter. Even though Philip was being used in a great way to the Samaritan people, God had even greater plans for him. This personal contact was probably his biggest revival campaign.

This story would be similar today of a missionary being sent out to a foreign mission field. Missionaries don't often know what they're going to encounter before they reach the field. Philip had no idea what God had planned for him until he met up with the eunuch, then it was very plain that he was to give the gospel to him. How little did Philip realize what great spiritual influence and blessing would come from his obedience.

We can readily see that Philip used spiritual wisdom in dealing with the eunuch's spiritual condition. We need to have spiritual discernment to the problems which perplex those to whom we are trying to win. God states in James 1:5 that we can have this wisdom according to the degree of our consecration to Christ. "If any of you lack wisdom, let him ask of God, that giveth to all men liberally, and upbraideth not; and it shall be given him."

I used to work the evening shift at a rehabilitation unit in Missouri. One evening as I was winding up my shift and just getting ready to give report to the on-coming nurse, I received a call from another unit asking me to help them out with a difficult intravenous insertion on a post-surgical patient. That particular night I was very tired and just wanted to finish up my work and go home, but the Holy Spirit had different plans for me.

As I was talking to the nurse from this other unit, I asked her to call the supervisor for help, as I was really busy with my own unit. The minute I hung up the phone I just knew I did wrong and I became very convicted. So I called her back, apologized for being so short with her, and told her I'd be right over when I finished giving report to the next shift.

When I was talking to the nurse on the phone the thought kept flashing through my mind that just maybe God was in this call. Isn't it amazing how we like to put God on our timetable, and not on His? It's fairly easy to serve God when everything is rosy and we're feeling great, but we tend to have second thoughts when our daily routine is interrupted. No matter how or when God calls us to serve Him, we just need to respond with a willing heart.

Carlos was a fifty-year-old man suffering from a bad infection from a recent back surgery. As I quickly introduced myself to him, I noticed he was reading a Bible. I made the comment that he was reading the greatest Book in the world.

As he laid the Bible on the bedside table, he sighed and made the comment, "I know it's a great book, but I wish I could understand what I'm reading." I took him off guard when I replied with a question, "Do you know the Author of the Book?" He said, "Well, maybe I don't. Can a person really know God?" I said, "Oh, yes, the Bible tells us how we can know Him in a personal way. After He comes into our lives, the Holy Spirit becomes our Teacher and enlightens our hearts as we read."

As I began to make preparations to insert the IV, he began to tell me his story: "The doctor said that I might not make it through the surgery as I was a poor surgical candidate. What he said scared me so bad that I asked the nurse to call for the Catholic priest. He came and said a few words over me, but after he left, I just didn't have any peace. But he did do one good thing before he left—he gave me this big Bible.

The night before surgery I didn't sleep at all. I clutched that Bible to my heart all night, hoping I could find some peace of mind. I knew in my heart that I wasn't ready to meet God and I was so frightened. Ever since, that Bible has been my good-luck charm."

I gently explained to Carlos that the Bible is not a good-luck charm, but it is God's love letter to mankind revealing Jesus as the Savior of sinners. He then told me that he was baptized into the Catholic Church as an infant, frequently confessed his sins to the priest, prayed to Mary, and went to mass frequently. He said he has never had any real joy or peace in his heart and couldn't understand why.

When I finished with the IV insertion, I asked him if I could show him from his Catholic Bible how to have peace with God. I could tell he was very eager to know how to be eternally saved, so I began in Ephesians 2:8, 9 where it says that our salvation is all by God's grace, not by our good works. "For by grace are ye saved through faith; and that not of yourselves; it is the gift of God: Not of works, lest any man should boast."

All his life he had been taught that faith in God plus doing all the church rituals would save him. I went on by saying, "If we could go to Heaven by our own merits, then there would not have been any reason for Jesus to die for our sins. He paid our sin debt in full when His precious blood was shed on the cross, and there's nothing we can add to that."

I showed him the verse in Romans 3:23 where it says, "For all have sinned and come short of the glory of God." As the old saying goes, "We need to get the person lost before we can get him saved." And that is so true as we are living in a time when it's not popular to talk about sin and repentance. I emphasized the word "all" in this verse as he was taught all his life that the Pope of Rome, and Mary, the mother of Jesus, were without sin. The Bible states very plainly that Mary acknowledged her sinfulness and her need of the Savior.

After I made sure that he understood he was a sinner, I showed him that because he was a sinner, he owed a sin debt, which is eternal Hell. I had him read Romans 6:23, "For the wages of sin is death..." I said, "Carlos, there is nothing we can do to pay that debt. But, the story doesn't end there, as there is a bright side to it. Look at the good news in Romans 5:8 where it says that Jesus paid your sin debt in full by shedding His precious blood for your sins. "But God commendeth his love toward us, in that, while we were yet sinners, Christ died for us."

Lastly, we read Romans 10:9, 10 where it tells how we can accept this wonderful gift of salvation: "That if thou shalt confess with thy mouth the Lord Jesus, and shalt believe in thine heart that God hath raised him from the dead, thou shalt be saved. For with the heart man believeth unto righteousness; and with the mouth confession is made unto salvation."

After I made sure that he understood the plan of salvation, I said, "Carlos, would you like to ask Jesus to be your personal Savior and cleanse you from your sins?" He replied, "Yes" before I could finish my sentence. With tears in his eyes he prayed the sinner's prayer, trusting in Jesus alone to save him.

After we lead a soul to Christ we always need to leave them with verses of assurance. This is so important as Satan works hard on new Christians to doubt their salvation. I usually use John 1:12 and John 3:36. Also, try to follow up with them after they're saved, encouraging them to be baptized and join a fundamental, Bible believing church where they can grow spiritually. This is so vital in their Christian growth.

I often think of this patient and how eager he was to know the truth of salvation. Remember, that sometimes God brings unknown opportunities to us when we least expect them, and sadly, we often miss out on them because we're not always sensitive to the leading of the Holy Spirit in our lives. If we are soul conscious, we will always be on the lookout on how to integrate the gospel in a conversation. In this instance, I made a positive comment on his Bible and that brought the conversation into spiritual avenues.

Oftentimes, before I retire for the night, I can hear that still, quiet voice of my Savior asking me if I made a difference in someone's life that day. If your day is like mine, every day is crammed full of tasks to get done. Sadly, I have to confess that many times I miss those divine appointments because I'm too focused on getting my earthly business done. With the story of Carlos, I thought of this opportunity at first as an inconvenience in my busy work schedule. Instead, I should have recognized this interruption right away as a divine appointment.

I wonder how many desperate people cross our path each day—people who are maybe one step away from destruction or people whose direction in life can be changed by the Lord through our interaction with them?

On your journey today, be on the lookout for those desperate ones who need you in their lives. Be a blessing by sowing into lives around you. God had uniquely equipped Philip to minister to this great man from Ethiopia. God has also uniquely equipped you for certain tasks that only you can do. Someone needs your gifts and talents that God has given you. Will you be available?

Chapter 8

UNUSUAL PLANS

"God adapts His will to our individual circumstances, and whether we realize it or not, we are always on call in His service." Dr. Charles Stanley

In the last chapter, we saw how the plans of God are often unknown and unexplained. The plans of God can also be unusual. In the story of Philip, God had certainly given him an unusual job to do. He was participating in a great revival in Samaria when God called him to leave what he was doing and go out into the desert and God doesn't even tell him why. God isn't under any obligation to give us all the "whys" in life. I like the way Dr. Charles Stanley puts it: "Obey God and leave all the consequences to Him."

In 2001 I had a real desire to do mission work in a third-world country, so I applied to a Traveling Nurse Agency. They gave me several countries to choose from: Hawaii, The Virgin Islands and the Island of Guam. After praying about it, I chose The Virgin Islands.

During the application process the Agency told me some very negative things about the hospital at St. Thomas and they tried to discourage me from going. They said it was most unusual for nurses to stay their allotted time of 13 weeks due to the poor wages and shortage of hospital nurses. But the cut in pay and the poor conditions of the hospital did not deter me from going as I was focusing on the mission work.

During my 13-week contract at the hospital I was amazed at what liberty I had to give the gospel to my patients. In fact, the hospital encouraged me to give out Christian literature as long as it was done discreetly.

All the native nurses knew that I had come to the Islands to help out in mission work; so I soon acquired the name, "missionary nurse," and whenever a patient requested spiritual help, they would call on me. Such was the case in the following story:

A co-worker told me that one of her patients was dying and the wife of the patient wanted someone to pray with her, so she asked me if I would talk to this lady.

Raquel was a very pretty, well-dressed lady from Puerto Rico that was very distressed about the condition of her husband. Oscar lay dying of cancer and was given just days to live. She shared with me that Oscar was the son of a very prominent African king.

After conversing with her she asked me if I would pray for her husband. I asked her if he had any religious background and if it was all right to share the gospel with him. I always find it helpful when witnessing to know first where that person is spiritually. She told me that he believed in God but was not a religious person, so I felt fairly confident that he was an unsaved man.

When dealing with dying patients, the soul winner needs to remember that their attention span is very short so words must be chosen very carefully, and the salvation message must be presented very simply. Also, of all the five senses, hearing is the last sense to go, so always take advantage of this and if need be, speak directly into their ear.

As I sat down beside Oscar, I could tell he was alert, but much too weak to talk. I took his hand in mine, introduced myself as a missionary nurse, and asked him if I could share the way to Heaven with him. He nodded his head, so I began to tell him very simply how to be saved. After I did this, I said, "Oscar, I'm now going to pray that you will believe on Jesus, repent of your sins, and accept Him into your heart. Then, I'll pray the words very slowly, and as I do this, you say the words in your heart, trusting Jesus to save you." He squeezed my hand, so I felt fairly confident that he understood and prayed the sinner's prayer in his heart.

The following is a format I use when dealing with dying patients, and sometimes it has to be modified to that particular patient, depending on how alert they are. The whole time the gospel is presented, you need to silently pray that the Holy Spirit will open their eyes to the truth as Satan has blinded the eyes of the unsaved. Until the blinders are lifted they won't be able to understand the glorious truth of the gospel.

- Jesus loves you and wants to give you eternal life.

- John 14:6—Emphasize that Jesus is the ONLY way to Heaven, as he may be trusting in his good works, baptism, or just a general belief in God for salvation.

- Romans 3:23—Make sure that he understands that he is a sinner in need of a Savior to forgive him.

- John 3:16—Make sure he understands the gospel: Jesus died personally for his sins and that He rose again the third day. Insert his name in this verse where it says, "whosoever." Emphasize that the word "believe" means to trust or accept Christ with the whole heart.

- Ask him to squeeze your hand if he would like to receive Christ and proceed like I did with Oscar. This is a sample prayer you can pray with him: Dear God: I know I'm a sinner, and I ask for your forgiveness. I realize that Christ's blood was shed to wash away my sins. I believe that You died and rose again for me and I receive You as my personal Savior. Please be merciful to me, a sinner. Thank you for saving me.

After leading a soul to Christ, always make sure you quote a verse of assurance. I like to use Romans 10:13 with these kind of people because it's very short and easy to understand. "For whosoever shall call upon the name of the Lord shall be saved."

If the dying person is un-responsive, do not give up. Keep in mind that God said in Isaiah 55:11, "So shall my word be that goeth forth out of my mouth; it shall not return unto me void..." Lean down to his ear and say, "God, be merciful to me a sinner." I'd repeat that a few times and pray he will hear and pray this prayer in his heart. Now, you may doubt that this will work, but always remember that while there is still life, there is hope, and remember that hearing is the last sense to leave a dying person.

Raquel thanked me for talking and praying with him, and before I left she said she had some questions and wanted to meet with me after work, so I told her I would meet with her at a certain time that day.

Raquel was waiting for me like she promised—her outgoing, bubbly personality made her a delight to be around. She told me that Oscar was getting specialized nursing care in the hospital where they lived in Puerto Rico, and had the best cancer specialists in the Caribbean. She said it didn't make sense that they would move him to the hospital in the Virgin Islands.

When she asked his doctor why he needed to be moved he could not give her a concrete answer. Then, she looked at me and said something I'll never forget. "Now, I know why—my husband needed to know how to be saved, and I need to know too." She then asked me if I would mind repeating what I told her husband. I was so moved by what she said that I could hardly speak.

I took my New Testament out of my lab coat pocket and God gave me the blessed privilege of leading this dear lady to the Lord. She shared with me that she never really thought about eternity until her husband was diagnosed with cancer. She had tried reading the Bible, but nothing made sense to her. The two hours I spent with her was a blessed time of fellowship—I could see the light of Jesus flooding her soul as I answered her questions from God's Word, and as we talked, I sensed a real desire in her to know more about spiritual things.

Going back to the story of Philip—he could have made all kinds of excuses not to obey God. Being a poor preacher, he could have been intimidated by this rich man driving that beautiful gold chariot. Or, he could have argued with God because the man was of a different race. But he didn't question God; he just obeyed Him and was so blessed because of his obedience.

John 2:5 gives us clear instruction in completely surrendering our lives to the Lord Jesus. "…Whatsoever he saith unto you, do it." Whenever He brings unsaved people into our paths, He's clearly giving us orders to give them the gospel. We always need to be at our Lord's disposal, whether we be at work, at school, or at the grocery store.

"Entire obedience to Christ brings the purest kind of joy…He makes Himself so clear, so near, so dear, to those who live to obey Him, that the very act of obeying becomes a joyous privilege.… Obedience is the eye of the spirit. Failure to obey dims and dulls the spiritual understanding.

As obedience continues, discernment develops, and knowledge of God expands. That inner, deeper understanding of divine things which some believers possess is always a by-product of obedience to Christ."[7]

Chapter 9

A LESSON FROM THE FLOWER

Like flowers, every person emits a scent—a fragrance that repels or one that attracts. Christians should emit the fragrance of Christ's love to a perishing world.

Have you ever wondered why God made beautiful flowers? Everything He made was good and for a definite reason. God is a God of beauty. We see in Genesis 1:2 that our world was dark and without form until God spoke beauty into it, and what a world of splendor, brilliance and grandeur it became.

In this chapter I want you to listen to what a beautiful flower is trying to tell you about the magnificence of our God and how we should respond to our Creator.

"You see, I was not always a pretty flower like this. I used to be an ugly brown seed, and it seemed as though nothing beautiful or worthwhile could ever come of ugly little me. What was worse, I was in utter darkness. All I knew was that I was down there, an ugly little seed, and could not see, and seemed to be dying without ever discovering why I was there at all. I don't know just how long I was there, but I began to feel a strange influence pulling me upwards. There was a power working in me, which I could not explain. I felt that somehow there must be something above me to which I must reach up.

Then, one morning when the sun had been shining for some time after rain-showers, I felt a wonderful power lift me right up; and suddenly I found myself in the light of a wonderful new world up here! After that I grew into the lovely flower at which you are looking; and now I gratefully bloom just for one thing—to "Show forth the praises of Him who called me out of darkness into His marvelous light."[8]

We were nothing but ugly, brown seeds lying dead in the cold ground. But, wait—there's good news. Jesus said in John 10:10, "I have come that they might have life, and that they might have it more abundantly." And the minute we repent of our sins and turn to Jesus, He immediately transfers us out of Satan's domain of darkness and places us into His glorious kingdom.

Just like the flower, there was a supernatural power in us that we couldn't explain, pulling us upward to discover the marvelous blessings that God has for us. All of a sudden, that power lifted us up to a new world where we can bathe in the light of God's love. The Apostle John in John 15:4 tells us to "Abide in Christ," and if we continue to abide in Him, He will make our lives beautiful and fragrant for His glory. And, like the flower, we will blossom for just one thing— for His honor and glory.

I love how Dr. J. Sidlow Baxter describes the new birth and I quote him; "Every true conversion to Christ is nothing less than a coming out of gross natural 'darkness' into a marvelous new spiritual 'light'—a transforming new discovery of God, and a world of spiritual realities unknown before."

Because God has made such a transition in our lives, should not we feel an obligation to show forth to others what He did in our lives? Those of us who have been rescued from the domain of darkness can bring a little bit of Heaven into the lives of people that are lost in sin. We have to realize that lost people are held captive by Satan until they accept Jesus into their lives.

While writing this book, I live in the hot desert of Nevada where you can travel for miles and all you see is cactus. All of a sudden you'll come upon a tall, beautiful flower that stands so stately among the thorns and weeds. That's the way we should be: A fragrant, radiant Christian blooming among the thorns of this world. There is not a higher calling than to "Show forth the praises of Him who hath called you out of darkness into His marvelous light!"

Years ago I worked with an older nurse in a hospital emergency room in my hometown in Idaho. We worked well together and became good friends. Judy was a person that spoke her mind and you always knew where you stood with her. One day she asked me, "You don't smoke or drink or do the party scene, so what makes you different—what do you do for fun?" So I had a chance to tell her that Christ made a difference in my life and my goal in life is to life for Him.

Judy had a daughter that was a Christian and was going to a fundamental Bible Church. I had spoken with her several times and she asked me if I would pray for her mother's salvation. So I told her I would and also told her that I had been witnessing to her.

One day when we had a quiet time at work, we were talking about life in general and she said, "Life just doesn't make a whole lot of sense—it just seems like we just exist with no real purpose in life." This opened the conversation up to spiritual avenues. I said, "Judy, until we understand that we are made by God and for God, life will never make sense and we will just exist. It's only in God that we discover our purpose."

Little by little, spiritual truths were sinking deep into her heart and I could tell by her questions that the Holy Spirit was working in her heart. She confided in me that she had lived a pretty wild life in her younger days and didn't think God would forgive her for some things she had done. I explained to her that we couldn't do anything to put ourselves beyond God's reach. I took her right to the story of the Prodigal Son and pointed out that the whole theme of the story is the love of our Heavenly Father towards the wayward sinner.

As we read the story together in Luke 15, we compared the earthly father with our Heavenly Father. After we read it, I said, "Judy, picture the Jewish father rising early every day, walking out to the gate, and gazing down the dusty road that held the painful memory of his wayward son. And, then, watch the father run to him with out-stretched arms, embracing the wandering son home. There were no angry, harsh words—only love and compassion. What a beautiful picture of God's amazing grace!"

Judy had tears in her eyes as we finished the story, and made the comment, "I've never seen that side of God before. In fact, I'm rather embarrassed to come to God as I've done some pretty bad things in my life." I reminded her, "No one can out sin the grace of our God. His very Name is compassion." Before we parted that day, she jotted down the reference to this story so she could look it up later to read. I silently prayed that God would touch her heart and lead her to repentance.

The longing of our Heavenly Father, gazing relentlessly down the road, never changes. It is so sad that He was and still is being rejected by ungrateful children that spurn His love for lives of sinful pleasure, but He is so overwhelmed with love and compassion for the wayward child that He constantly pursues us. He always has, and He always will. As long as there is life, He'll be standing at the gate watching and waiting for the penitent child to come home.

Sometime later Judy had elective surgery done. The night before surgery, I went to visit her. I didn't stay long, but prayed and read Scripture with her and just wanted to let her know that I cared about her. I hugged her and told her that our church would be praying for her.

Her surgery went well, and just before she was discharged from the hospital, Joyce, my pastor's wife, and I visited her in the hospital and before we left, Judy came to know Jesus as her own personal Savior. She told me later that she didn't know why she waited so long to be saved. Then, she said something that really stuck with me and taught me to be always loving and patient to those I'm trying to win. She said, "You and the church people really were concerned and didn't give up on me."

After her conversion, she started attending her daughter's church and eventually became an active member. I slowly noticed a change in her at work—she still had worldly habits to overcome, but there was a sincere desire to learn the Word of God and be obedient to the One who saved her.

If there is no desire to sit at the feet of Jesus and be fed the Bread of Life, then there is something drastically wrong with our professing faith. I've seen many professing Christians that at one time had prayed a prayer for salvation, but looking at their lives, there was no visible signs of a new life in Christ. Jesus said in Matthew 3:8, "Bring forth therefore fruits meet for repentance." In other words, "Let your lives prove your change of heart."

Galatians 5:22 & 23 tell us that the "fruits" mentioned in Matthew 3:8 are "...love, joy, peace, patience, gentleness, goodness, faith, meekness, and temperance;..." Each "fruit" is a different aspect of Christ-likeness. In the Gospels, we see how Christ was our example in all these virtues. Now, He wants to see them at work in each of our lives. These character traits, or I like to call them "ornaments of grace," are proof that God is at work in our lives.

"Fruitfulness for Christ depends on fellowship with Christ."
D. DeHaan

Chapter 10

WHAT ARE YOU ADDICTED TO?

"I do not know if there is a more dreadful word in the English language than that word "lost."
Charles Spurgeon

When we hear the word "addicted" we automatically think of people being addicted to drugs and alcohol. I think of it as a dark plague that has literally destroyed the minds and bodies of countless people, mainly young people.

Destructive addictions to alcohol, marijuana, cocaine, heroin, methamphetamines, and strong prescription pain pills have reached a turning point in our society. It's heartbreaking to see so many decent, well-respected people sink so low in this mire of sin. What they don't realize is that Satan is holding them captive, and they will be utterly destroyed unless the glorious light of the gospel penetrates their hearts.

Please stop and get into your mind a clear picture of the monstrous tragedy of sin and what it means for a soul to be lost in Hell forever. Sin is really sin, and Hell is no fiction. Revelation 21:8 tells us that sorcerers will have their place in the lake of fire. "Sorcerers" in the Greek translate into our English as "pharmacy" or "drugs." My friend, I hope the eternal consequences of sin alarm you. We should do everything in our power to keep our friends and loved ones from this horrible pit of destruction.

The following story is an example of how the Lord taught me to be very patient and faithful while witnessing to a close friend that kept resisting the gospel. As the farmer sows the seed in the ground, he needs to be patient. As we sow seeds of eternal life, there is going to be resistance, hostility and sometimes, no reaction at all. Always remember that it takes time to go from planting to harvest. God has His timing with every person, and what seems like a failure now might become a victory later.

Donna worked the night shift with me on the medical-surgical floor in a small hospital in Missouri. She was a very bright, intelligent, likable lady whose main goal in life was to get her BSN degree in nursing; and she did this by both working and going to school on a full-time basis.

It was very obvious that she was addicted to drugs, especially marijuana. Many times I would pick her up for work only to have my car reek of a joint that she had just smoked. Donna lived with her boyfriend who constantly abused her mentally and physically. He was a very talented painter, but the money he made all went on drugs and alcohol.

I remember one evening our church was out on visitation and we happened to be in her neighborhood, so we stopped by and paid her a visit. As we approached her house we heard loud rock music and partying coming from the house. After several knocks at the door she and her boyfriend answered, both very high on drugs. The air was so thick with marijuana that the smell literally made me nauseous.

That visit made me more determined than ever to win my friend to the Lord. I knew that Satan held her captive in his clutch, and she would not be free from this horrible addiction unless she repented and accepted Christ as her Savior.

After months of witnessing to her she consented to come to a church service with me. That Sunday my pastor delivered a powerful gospel message, and at the invitation time I said, "Donna, would you like to be saved?" I could tell she was under conviction, but she shook her head, and said, "Not now, there's so much in my life to give up."

The soul winner needs to be very sensitive in this area of putting the pressure on people to be saved, because we don't want a premature and un-real decision. We have to realize that the Holy Spirit is in the process of "wooing" them to the Father, and instead of putting pressure on them, we need to continue to intercede that they will come to the knowledge of the truth.

Even though we are not to pressure people to make a decision for Christ, at the same time, we are to plead with them by telling them the consequences of repeatedly rejecting Jesus. 2 Corinthians 5:11 tells us, "...Knowing therefore the terror of the Lord, we persuade men." Keep in mind that opportunities are often here just for a day, an hour, and then are gone forever.

We need to remember that each time a person refuses to make a decision for Christ, it continues the process of hardening the heart against spiritual things. 2 Corinthians 6:2 says, "...behold, now is the accepted time; behold, now is the day of salvation." Matthew Henry states, "The present time is the only proper season to accept of the grace that is offered...the morrow is none of ours; we know not what will be on the morrow."

"Let us seize opportunities of winning souls for Christ while we may. D. L. Moody tells how he gave an evangelistic address to a large Chicago audience, and then told them to go home and think carefully about accepting Jesus as Savior. Before the next Sunday came, the great Chicago fire occurred. Many of those people were burned to death, and many others Moody never saw again. After that, whenever he preached the Gospel, he always pleaded for immediate decision."[9]

I never gave up on Donna. I knew that God placed her in my path and I wasn't about to let Satan have the victory in her life. The combination of working, school, drugs, alcohol, and living in an unhealthy environment gradually took its toll on her to the point where she became suicidal. After being counseled by my pastor, she left her abusive boyfriend and enrolled in a drug-rehabilitation program.

For months our church prayed for her, and after about a year she started coming to our Bible classes. One night after Bible study, I had the privilege of leading Donna to the Lord. As I was showing her how to be saved, she shared with me, "Helen, I thought I had to first clean up my life before God would accept me." I told her, "No, we need to come to Jesus just as we are, and He forgives us of all our sins and wipes the slate clean. God uses His heavenly eraser that deletes every wrong deed and wipes every sin off the blackboard. And, of course, that eraser is the precious blood of Christ."

I showed her Isaiah 1:18 where it declares, "...though your sins be as scarlet, they shall be as white as snow..." As Donna read this verse she said, "Yes, I can certainly identify with this verse—my sins were very scarlet!" Together we read another verse in Psalm 103:12, "As far as the east is from the west, so far hath he removed our transgressions from us." I said to her, "Donna, I so love this verse—meditate on it. You can go east as far as you can, and it will never go west. God not only forgives, but He also forgets."

Oh, what soul winners we should prayerfully attempt to be! How unconcerned some of us are. How seldom we get enough courage to warn our friends of the wrath to come. With cords of love we should do every thing possible to draw them to the Savior.

"Every God-conscious human soul is a world in itself, with immeasurable possibilities for good or evil, in time and eternity. When a soul falls deeply away from God, demons beat the gongs of darkness. When a soul is saved through union with God's dear Son, Heaven sounds its trumpets in joyful fanfare; eager fingers pluck new strains of gladness from a thousand harps; and all the belfries peal out jubilation!"[10]

Just as there are addictions to evil things, there is also a positive connotation to addiction. According to the dictionary, the word means "a compelling motivation." A good example of this would be the famous jungle pilot, Nate Saint, who became a missionary to the killer tribe of the Auca Indians in Ecuador.

His life was focused on one thing—to take the gospel to a people that had never heard the name of Jesus. Nate knew that there is only one thing worth expending one's life for—living out the Great Commission.

Thousands of Christians have given their lives into fulltime service in the Lord's work, and have become addicts for the sake of the gospel. Sometimes members in our own families will not understand the stand we take for the Lord. They may find that the cost of obedience seems too high, or they may have turned back and said, "This is not for me." But we need to ask them, "What about the cost of disobedience?"

My friend, what about you? Do you realize that God has given every believer a special gift to share with others? There are people in your little corner of the world that will only respond to you. Your mission field is wherever God has placed you.

I encourage you to be an addict for good. Don't ever give up on people. Be passionate for the cause of Christ. The Lord loves it when we get passionate about the souls of men. Nothing is more satisfying than being that human instrument God uses to bring a lost soul to a saving knowledge of Christ.

Chapter 11

LORD, GIVE ME MORE ELSIES

God works through your personality and faithfulness to draw others into His kingdom. We are to faithfully sow the precious Word of Life and look for those who are ripe for harvest.

Every time I think of Elsie, it brings joy to my heart. She is a prime example of someone who is "Ripe for harvest." Let me take you into Elsie's hospital room in Joplin, Missouri, and share with you what God did in her life.

Elsie was a sixty-year-old schoolteacher recovering from a major hip operation. I was assigned to her the two weeks she was at the hospital, and what a joy it was to be her nurse. It seemed that right away we bonded as nurse and patient, and it was that bond that made it very easy for me to witness to her.

Elsie shared a room with another patient who was also recovering from surgery. Mary was a very sweet Christian that had very poor eyesight, so when I had extra time I would read to her from a devotional book. Almost every day we would have a precious time of Christian fellowship.

One day as I was changing Elsie's hip dressing, she asked if I had any extra booklets that I had read to her roommate. I always kept extra ones in my pocket so I was delighted to give it to her. Because I didn't have any extra time to visit that day, I encouraged her to read the booklet, especially the first two pages that gave the plan of salvation, and I told her I'd be back the following day.

When I returned the next day I found Elsie full of questions and very eager to know the truth about being "saved." She had stayed up late the night before and had read the whole book. I came back on my lunch break, sat down with her, and tried to answer her questions.

She confessed to me that all her life had been totally focused on her teaching career, and even though she believed in God, she had left Him out of her life. Like so many people, Elsie had a lot of worldly wisdom, but God tells us to seek that divine wisdom that only comes from above. Like I told Elsie, "Acceptance of Jesus into our life is the beginning of true wisdom."

This dear lady really blessed my heart. She would write down all the references of the salvation verses that I gave her so she could look them up later. After I gave her a clear-cut presentation of the gospel I could tell she was very eager to be saved, so right there in that hospital bed she repented of her sins, and accepted Christ into her life.

When I came back to work the next day Elsie said, "Helen, because this is all so new to me, I want to go over the plan of salvation again. I want to make sure I did everything just right to be saved." I couldn't help but smile because I knew that Elsie, being a strict schoolteacher, had to be sure that everything she did was done exactly right.

She said, "I'm not so sure if I repented enough to be really saved." I replied by saying, "Repentance is a change of attitude toward sin and toward God. In the Greek it literally means 'a change of mind.' Repentance does not mean just nodding in agreement with what God's Word says, and then continue the same way we were going. We can experience instantaneous salvation when we turn with believing hearts to Jesus."

I went over the plan of salvation with her again, and this time the gospel became clearer to her, and she had the assurance that she was saved.

I went on to explain to her that repentance and faith are two sides of the same coin. One who turns from sin in repentance turns to Christ in faith. Then, I gave her a good example of this with the Philippian jailer in Acts 16 where he had beaten Paul and Silas and put them into prison. After God intervened with an earthquake, the jailer threw himself at the feet of Paul and Silas, and begged them to tell him the way of salvation.

The Bible says immediately after he was saved, he was a changed man. And his actions showed this by taking Paul and Silas to his house, washed their bleeding backs, and gave them a meal. He turned immediately from being a persecutor of Christians to a servant of the Lord.

When we truly agree with God about what is right, then, our behavior will follow. Like a car, we go in the direction we are pointed. The jailer is a good example of someone that has true saving faith, because not every one that makes a profession of faith is a true believer.

True saving faith will always result in a life of obedience. That's the meaning of the salvation verse in Romans 10:9-10, "For with the heart man believeth unto righteousness..." Notice here that God didn't say "with the mind"—it has to come from the heart. It is a deep heart belief that leads to a life of righteousness. This does not mean that the Christian will never sin, but it means that there will be a sincere desire to love and please the Lord.

I like what A.W. Tozer says as he touches on this unpopular subject of repentance:

"The idea that God will pardon a rebel who has not given up his rebellion is contrary both to the Scriptures and to common sense. How horrible to contemplate a church full of persons who have been pardoned but who still love sin and hate the ways of righteousness. And how much more horrible to think of Heaven as filled with sinners who had not repented nor changed their way of living...The teaching of salvation without repentance has lowered the moral standards of the church and produced a multitude of deceived religious professors who erroneously believe themselves to be saved when in fact they are still in the gall of bitterness and the bond of iniquity."[11]

Elsie shared with me that she had never heard the gospel story before. She said she had an older brother that went to a Baptist Church all his life, but had never invited her to go, and had never so much as given her a gospel tract. How tragic! But before we judge her brother too severely, we need to look at our own hearts. How many times has God put people in our path that we know we should witness to or at least give them a gospel tract, and we refuse to do it. Every day we need to ask God to stamp "Eternity" in our hearts for the lost.

I never will forget Elsie and her eagerness and sincerity to know the truth, and the desire to do explicitly what the Word of God said. Oh, how I pray every day that God would lead me to more people that would be as sincere as Elsie was about her soul.

May this poem by Fannie Crosby encourage you to win souls for our Lord:

> "When the voice of the Master is calling,
> And the gates of the city unfold,
> When the saints arise in His likeness
> And are thronging the City of Gold—
> How your heart shall rejoice in that morning,
> If one of the ransomed shall say,
> You guided my footsteps to Heaven—
> You told me of Jesus, the Way."

Chapter 12

A DOUBLE BLESSING

We're responsible for building meaningful bridges to unsaved people. When God gives us those golden opportunities, be willing to share with others how Christ has worked in your life and what He's able to do in theirs.

In the previous chapter I wrote of a dear lady that earnestly wanted to know how to become a child of God, and wanted to make sure that she did everything just right. Just recently I've thought a lot about Elsie, and have been earnestly pleading with God to bring more "Elsies" into my life.

I truly believe that the soul winner must be a master of the art of prayer. We cannot bring souls to God if we do not go to God ourselves. If we are much alone with Jesus, we will catch His passion for the lost. There is a precious promise found in Ephesians 3:20, and as I earnestly prayed, I reminded God of His promises to His children. "Now unto him that is able to do exceeding abundantly above all that we ask or think, according to the power that worketh in us."

Does He not also say in Psalm 81:10, "…open thy mouth wide, and I will fill it?" God loves it when we remind Him of His promises to us and when we're willing to prove Him to be true in our lives.

Another blessed promise is found in Mark 11:24, "... What things soever ye desire, when ye pray, believe that ye receive them, and ye shall have them..." In other words, "Have what your faith expects" or "Be it unto you according to your faith."

Recently, God gave me a wonderful answer to prayer— He just didn't give me one blessing, but He gave me a double blessing! It was a quiet day at work, as we weren't expecting any new admissions. However, things changed quickly, and we admitted a patient from the hospital outpatient department.

When I looked at the patient and then at the admission papers, I couldn't believe my eyes—there, in front of me was a lady in a wheelchair with the name of "Elsie," and with the same last name as the lady in my previous chapter. Right away, I could see the hand of God all through this admission.

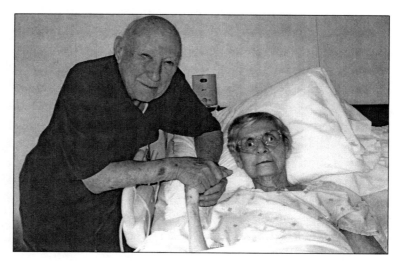

Warren and Elsie Frank, Las Vegas, Nevada

Elsie had cancerous tumors in her lungs, and had just undergone a procedure that would drain fluid from her lungs. I knew I'd be spending a lot of nursing time with her, as I would be the one to hook her lung catheter up to a drainage system every day.

Elsie was very alert and was still well enough to walk short distances with assistance. Her husband, Warren, stayed with her at night, and was a big help in her care. Like the "other Elsie," we began to bond very quickly, and I began to silently pray that I could be an effective witness to her and her husband.

One day as I was changing her chest dressing, I noticed a book by Dr. Robert Schuller of the Crystal Cathedral on her bedside table. She shared with me that her and her husband usually watched him every Sunday, and then she asked me what I thought of him.

I answered her question with a question. I said, "Elsie, has Dr. Schuller ever told you the way to Heaven from the Bible?" She thought for a moment, and then said, "Well, no, he just talks like everyone is going to Heaven." I said, "Exactly, that's because he preaches a social gospel. He does not believe that mankind has a sinful nature and is in need of a Savior."

She then asked me what I meant by a "social gospel," so I had the privilege of telling her and her husband the true gospel story. I shared with them how Jesus saved me at the young age of nine, and what a wonderful Savior He has been to me down through the years.

In my pocket I had a gospel tract with that famous picture of Jesus knocking at the door. I asked them both if they knew the significance of the picture. They just thought it was a beautiful picture. I explained to them that it was more than a beautiful picture, as it meant that Jesus was sent into this world "...To seek and to save that which was lost" (Luke

19:10). He patiently knocks at the door of our hearts to let Him in.

By showing them Revelation 3:20, the light began to dawn upon their hearts. "Behold, I stand at the door and knock; if any man hear my voice, and open the door, I will come into him, and will sup with him, and he with me."

Showing them the picture, I asked, "Do you notice anything unusual about the door?" Right away Warren spoke up and said, "Why, yes, there's no doorknob on the outside." So, I told them, "Jesus did His part by taking all your sins on Him at Calvary so that you might be forgiven. Now, He is knocking at your heart's door to let Him in, but He is a gentleman, and won't force His way in."

I continued by saying, "I want you both to read this verse again and pay particular attention to the words, 'hear' and 'open.' First, we have to hear the gospel message so the Holy Spirit can convict our hearts of sin. Then, we need to make a choice whether or not we're going to respond and open our hearts to Him."

I said, "Remember, the doorknob is on the inside—only you can open up the door of your heart." That day, this precious husband and wife bowed their heads, asked Jesus to forgive them of their sins, and accepted Christ as their personal Savior.

I like what Matthew Henry says about this verse: "Christ is graciously pleased by His word and Spirit to come to the door of the heart of sinners. He finds this door shut against him; the heart of man is by nature shut up against Christ. When he finds the heart shut, he does not immediately withdraw, but he waits to be gracious. Those who open to him shall enjoy his presence."[12]

I shared with them that there is a "Book of Life" in Heaven, and as they trusted Christ as their personal Savior, their names were written in that Book. They looked at me in amazement and asked if that was really in the Bible. The

Apostle John tells us in Revelation 20:15, "And whosoever was not found written in the book of life was cast into the lake of fire." I could tell that their souls were so starved of spiritual truths and it was such a blessed privilege to share the things of Christ with them.

Don't tell me that God doesn't answer the cries for soul winning power in the life of the believer. I believe with all my heart that "IMPORTUNITY" (persistence or boldness) in praying is the way to get things from God.

Jesus gave us this story in Luke 11:5-8 regarding this very thing, "Which of you shall have a friend, and shall go unto him at midnight, and say unto him, Friend, lend me three loaves; For a friend of mine in his journey is come to me, and I have nothing to set before him? And he from within shall answer and say, 'Trouble me not: the door is now shut, and my children are now with me in bed; I cannot rise and give thee.' I say unto you, Though he will not rise and give him, because he is his friend, yet because of his importunity he will rise and give him as many as he needeth."

As the midnight caller suggests, Christ is the bread and food we are to ask for in the lives of other people. This story instructs us to come boldly to our God, asking shamelessly and audaciously. We are to pray intimately, knowing that when we ask, seek, and knock, it is our Heavenly Father that will open the door.

I believe that the Christian who wants the supernatural, miracle-working power of the Holy Spirit has a right to wait on God and plead for soul winning power. This power is only given to those who learn the secret of importunity. Persistence in prayer is one way of getting God's attention.

God is holding out the golden scepter to each of us, and is just waiting for us to touch it with our cries to Him. God's formula for getting answers to pray is very simple: We should always pray and not give up. Just think what a difference you would make in many unsaved lives if you were to pray passionately and faithfully for their salvation.

Do you realize that a soul winner is called a "Birther for God?" The Holy Spirit uses a physical happening like childbirth to describe a spiritual happening. When we travail in earnest prayer, like mothers travail in childbirth, then God will birth new life in that particular individual. The writer of Isaiah 66:7, 8 tells us, "...for as soon as Zion travailed, she brought forth her children." We cannot produce spiritual people, but our travail can.

Maybe I'm addressing someone who has persistently prayed for years regarding a certain individual—maybe a loved one or a close friend. We need to remember that sometimes prayer for a human being can be a long process.

I have learned to claim the promise in James 5:16 where it says, "...The effectual fervent prayer of a righteous man availeth much." The word, "fervent," means, "glowing hot, zealous, vehement." The Lord loves it when we get boiling hot and glowing in our cries to Him. I truly think that many times our prayers have no power because they have no heart. If we don't put much heart in our prayers, why would you expect God to answer them?

"Men may spurn our appeals, reject our message, oppose our arguments, despise our persona, but they are helpless against our prayers." J. Sidlow Baxter.

May the following words from Oswald Chambers encourage your heart in the area of intercession for the unsaved: "When we pray for others the Spirit of God works in the unconscious domain of their being that we know nothing about, and the one we are praying for knows nothing about. But after the passing of time the conscious life of the one prayed for begins to show signs of unrest and disquiet. We may have spoken until we are worn out, but we have never come anywhere near, and we have given up in despair. But if we have been praying, we find on meeting them one day that there is the beginning of a softening and a desire to know something.

It is that kind of intercession that does the most damage to Satan's kingdom. It is so slight, so feeble in its initial stages, that if our reason is not wedded to the light of the Holy Spirit, we will never do it. Yet it is that kind of intercession that the New Testament places the most emphasis on. It seems stupid to think that we can pray and all that will happen. But remember to whom we pray. We pray to a God who understands the unconscious depths of personality about which we know nothing, and He has told us to pray. The Great Master of the human heart said, '...Greater works than these he will do...And whatever you shall ask in My name, that will I do... (John 14:12-13)."[13]

Chapter 13

SOMEONE IS WATCHING YOU

"Do not be discouraged while soul winning. Always keep at it and look for the one who is looking for you."
Jack Trieber

When was the last time you shared the gospel with someone? The Christian life is not meant to be hoarded, but shared. When you step out in faith and share the Good News, you receive the favor of God. Proverbs 11:25 tells us that "The liberal soul shall be made fat: and he that watereth shall be watered also himself."

We all have a story to tell of how God changed our lives, and we have a duty to share the gospel with that special person God places in our path. Don't let your testimony lie dormant—God wants to do a miracle through you. Always remember that when we share the Word of God and pray fervently for others, then their eyes will be opened to His love.

The following story is about a close co-worker that the Lord gave me the privilege of leading to Him. When you win someone to Christ, especially a close friend, it's a joy that's hard to describe. Your wedding day is exciting. Your first baby is exciting, but the most thrilling thing you can ever do is win someone to the Lord.

I worked with Marsha in a hospital in Central Idaho. She usually worked in the ICU right next to the surgical floor where I worked. Our friendship was one that she initiated and one of those situations where it was so obvious that it was God that brought us together.

I was in the break-room one evening when Marsha came in to join me. I really didn't know her, but somehow she knew I was a Christian and that I went to church every Sunday. As we were getting acquainted she mentioned she had been watching me pick up her neighbor every Sunday for church, and wanted to know which church I attended. I told her I was going to a Baptist Church that was just getting started.

We became good friends, had quite a bit in common, and best of all, she and her two small children started coming to church with me. One day we took our children on a picnic and as they were playing she brought up the subject of the Bible. She wasn't raised in a Christian home and spiritual things were new to her.

As I tried to answer her questions she said she felt that something was lacking in her life—she had a lovely family, a nursing degree, a good job; but she felt that there was more to life than all these things. I knew what she was lacking and I began to tell her about the abundant life that Jesus gives to those who trust Him as Lord and Savior.

While showing her the plan of salvation, I brought in the 3 R'S of salvation:

- Realize all have sinned—We must be willing to repent of our sins.

- Recognize Jesus as Lord—We must believe that Jesus is God and He, alone can save.

- Receive the Resurrected Savior—We must be willing to receive Christ into our life with our whole heart.

Before the picnic was over Marsha asked Jesus to be her Savior. It was such a joy seeing her come to know the Lord and it was even a greater joy to see her grow in spiritual things. Right after she was saved she asked me, "Is God supposed to give me some special feeling? I knew a lady that said she received some "religious experience" when she was saved."

I told her, "God says very little about feelings, but He mentions 'faith' and 'believe' many times in regards to salvation. So, evidently God considers these to be far more important than our feelings."

Then we discussed what feelings really are. I said, "Marsha, let me use your marriage as an illustration—sometimes you may feel married, sometimes you may not. But that doesn't change the fact that you're married. It's the same way with salvation. If our salvation is based on our feelings, then we would be forever on an emotional roller coaster and we would have a very shaky faith. There's no eternal hope in our changeable feelings, but our hope is based on the facts of the eternal Word of God."

I shared with Marsha that there were times in my Christian life that I had doubts about my salvation and I didn't feel saved, but they came at times when I was out of fellowship with my Heavenly Father. So I learned through the years to claim two wonderful verses that helped me so much. Romans 10:17 states, "So then faith cometh by hearing, and hearing by the word of God." The other one is I John 1:9, "If we confess our sins, he is faithful and just to forgive us our sins, and to cleanse us from all unrighteousness."

I went on to explain to her that when we are out of fellowship with our Lord, then our minds will be nothing but a playground for Satan. We always need to keep short accounts with God—always confessing our sins so we can be in fellowship with Him. I showed her Psalm 119:11 that I memorized early in my Christian life, "Thy word have I hid in mine heart, that I might not sin against thee."

About nine months later her and her family moved to Colorado to be close to her father who was in failing health. Later she called to tell me that her father became a Christian before he died. She requested prayer for her husband and also for her mother that were still unsaved. I encouraged her by reminding her of the precious promises of God, one of which is found in Acts 16:31, "...Believe on the Lord Jesus Christ, and thou shalt be saved, and thy house." I told her that God wants to save her family more than she wants them saved, and to keep on trusting and interceding for them.

We kept in touch over the years until I heard of her death in 2007. This came as a shock to me as she was always so full of life and it was very hard to imagine her gone. I grieve for her because I'll miss the fellowship we shared, but I have tears of joy that she's enjoying the summerland of Heaven, never again to suffer the pain of cancer. I rejoice that her name is written in the Lamb's Book of Life and that someday we will meet again.

As I look back over our close friendship, I came to realize that God brings certain people into our lives for just a season, and then He moves us on. Our work is finished in their lives, the need has been met, and we need to thank the Lord that He allowed us to be a part of their lives. And knowing them has made our lives richer and fuller.

Do you realize that our lives are made visible by God's choice? Some Christians would prefer to lead private lives and be more exclusive in what others know about them. But I believe that God has other ideas. God is trying to save a world that does not know Him.

2 Corinthians 5:20 says it all: "...we are ambassadors for Christ..." Webster's Dictionary defines an ambassador as a representative of the highest rank. I don't think most Christians really understand what it is to be the King's

ambassador. It is one thing to be the child of the Most High God, but it is something that is very honorable to be an ambassador.

I believe the Apostle Paul is writing about all this in 2 Corinthians 3:2-3…"You are our letter…known and read by all men…you are a letter of Christ." We need to live with the awareness that others are watching and learning from us. When the anointing of the Lord is upon us, we cannot be careless with any part of our lives. We have to remember that it's all about Jesus, not us.

There are many things that can cause us to be careless in our Christian testimony. Things such as skipping our private devotions before we start the day can be very detrimental to our Christian witness. Do you know what we're really doing when we have a quiet time every day? We're actually weeding the garden of our minds and hearts, so the good seed of the Word of God can take root and grow.

God is constantly trying to plant new seeds in your heart, and your heart is the soil for those seeds. Listen to the words of wisdom in Proverbs 4:23, "Keep thy heart with all diligence; for out of it are the issues of life." God, who gave us these souls, gave us a strict charge with them, and we should watch what we permit our hearts to dwell on. We need to keep out bad thoughts that will defile our hearts with sin.

I have found that giving our life to the Lord is a daily choice and a daily taking up our cross and following Jesus. Every day we must say to Him, "Lord, I am your child. Everything that I have –body, soul, money, children, and spouse—all that I am and have belong to You." We must allow the Holy Spirit to take God's Word and weave it into every fiber of our being. The heart of the dedicated Christian longs to be obedient to His God.

Another sin that hurts our testimony is forgetting to worship with other believers as often as we can. "Not forsaking the assembling of ourselves together, as the manner of some is;" The author of Hebrews commands us, "but exhorting one another: and so much the more, as ye see the day approaching" (Hebrews 10:25). And, of course, "That day" speaks of His coming.

So many Christians let worldly things crowd out this command that God has given us. We need each other in a church setting for fellowship and to build each other up in the things of God—there is no such thing as individual Christianity. Marsha saw that church attendance and picking people up for church was a priority in my life and she wanted to see why it was so important.

Unsaved people should notice a difference in our conduct when comparing us to the rest of the world. Are they seeing Biblical principles at work in our lives? We shouldn't tell our friends and neighbors that we love Jesus and then take off for the beach or the mountains every weekend. They will see that we don't love Him enough to obey Him, and friends, if we truly love the Lord with all our hearts, we will do what He says in His Word. Always remember, "Obedience gives birth to blessings." How true that is—I've seen those blessings in my life and in the lives of other Christians.

Enoch in the Old Testament is an example of a godly person who had a vibrant witness and testimony for the Lord in a time characterized by sexual perversion and uncontrolled violence. He was watched and observed by the ungodly during a unique time in history, just before God's judgment came by the flood.

Moses tells us, "Enoch lived sixty-five years, and begot Methuselah:...And Enoch walked with God: and he was not; for God took him" (Genesis 5:21-24). Against this very dark background we see a man who walked with God and was spared death.

Enoch is a picture of believers that are living at the time when Jesus returns for His own, called the Rapture. He's also an example of how believers should be living when the

Rapture occurs. I want to look at some secrets from his life that we can apply to our lives as well.

First of all, Enoch was well pleasing to God. Hebrews 11:5 says, "...he had this testimony, that he pleased God." He pleased God because he was in close communion with him on a daily basis. He was entirely dead to this world, and did not only walk after God, but he walked with God, as if he was already in Heaven. We read of his glorious removal to a better world—he did not live like the rest, and he did not die like the rest. I like what Matthew Henry says regarding this, "Those whose conversation in the world is truly holy shall find their removal out of it truly happy."

Then, Enoch was a witness for his Lord. What does the word, "witness" mean? It simply means to testify or to give evidence. In order to testify, we have to open our mouths and tell people what the Lord has done for us. The Bible doesn't say, but I just imagine Enoch was a preacher like Noah. What a glorious testimony he had for the Lord.

Another Biblical example of a person being watched by the unsaved world was that of the seraphic Stephen. We read in the book of Acts that as Stephen preached to these proud, religious people, they "...saw his face as it had been the face of an angel" (Acts 6:15). We read that Saul of Tarsus (later, his name was changed to the Apostle Paul) was among this godless crowd and was the instigator of his death. While the stones were whirling through the air at Stephen, Paul witnessed Stephen praying for his persecutors. What a witness that must have been! No wonder Stephen had such a tremendous impact upon him.

I don't think any of us will be stoned to death, but as the ungodly world watches our lives, I wonder what they see? Do they see Christ in us? Do they see in us a real desire to serve the Lord, or do they see a lukewarmness in our Christian testimony? Revelation 3:16 tells us what happens to those professing people that are lukewarm. "So then because thou art lukewarm, and neither cold nor hot; I will spew thee out of my mouth." In other words, if we are not on fire for God, He said He would rather prefer us to be cold instead of lukewarm. And He pictures Himself as vomiting us out of His mouth because of this sin. These are strong words coming from the lips of our Savior. Jesus makes no apology for demanding obedience from His children.

Chapter 14

REDEEMING YOUR TIME

"The clock of life is wound but once, and no man has the power to tell just when the hands will stop—At late or early hour. NOW is the only time you own; Live, love, toil with a will. Place no faith in tomorrow for the clock may then be still."
Author Unknown

In the light of our calling to win others to a saving knowledge of Christ, I would like to share a few thoughts on the importance of using our time wisely. God has given each of us a valuable treasure—a lifetime of unlimited opportunities.

What would you do if you found out that you have only one year to live? I'm sure that most people would make sure that final year was packed full of meaningful activities with those you love. We all want to have lives that are full and fruitful. When we come to the end of life, we don't want to feel like we've wasted our time on insignificant things. We want our lives to count. So let's take a look at what the Bible says about what we can do to make our lives more meaningful.

As I grow older in the Lord, I've found that I get more joy out of things I've done for others than from the things I receive. The Bible repeatedly tells us that those who bless others will be blessed themselves, not only here on earth, but also in Heaven. Look at the wonderful promise found in Luke 6:38, "Give, and it shall be given unto you; good measure, pressed down, and shaken together, and running over, shall men give into your bosom. For with the same measure that ye mete withal it shall be measured to you again." This not only speaks of giving of our money, but also giving of our time.

Each of us is given a definite life span. Psalm 139:16 states "And in thy book all my members were all written, which in continuance were fashioned, when as yet there was none of them." In Heaven, we'll have no limitations; but here on earth we have only so many years, days, hours, and seconds. Since time management is very important to God, we need to view it as a spiritual discipline.

Do you realize that every hour of every day is either wasted or invested? No balance is carried into the next day and every night erases what we fail to use. If we use it in the wrong way, then, that time is lost forever and cannot be reclaimed. Today, examine your time management habits in the light of eternity. Initiate schedule changes that honor the Lord and make a new commitment to invest your time wisely. Always remember that we either set our life priorities or we allow circumstances and people to set them.

One of the most incredible gifts that God has given to us is "time." Paul writes in the book of Ephesians, "Redeeming the time, because the days are evil"—The world is occupied with the enjoyment of sin and selfish pleasure. In the Greek, the word "time" means "opportunity," or "seasons of time." You may never have thought of this, but we are not the owner of time—God is the owner. Every day is a precious gift from God and, if that being the case, then, we are stewards of the time that He gives us.

I want to dwell on two aspects of time: First, time is a "present opportunity." Every morning we need to prioritize our time by reserving a part of our morning in feeding our starving souls the Bread of Life. I read of a missionary that was trying to get the importance of this across to the native people. He explained it this way: "Lord Jesus, make my heart sit down." Solitude is deliberately setting aside time to "sit down" at the feet of Jesus. It's in those still, quiet moments of solitude that we hear God's voice and gain strength and wisdom for that particular day. Some of us wouldn't think of starting the day without a cup of delicious coffee—how much more important it is to feed our souls.

As we lift our hearts in prayer we need to ask the Lord to direct our steps into avenues of service for that day, not for tomorrow or next year because they may never come. Focus your prayers on the here and now. Personally, I have found that just spending a short time in His presence convinces me that Jesus is a lover of precious souls. It is impossible to seek His face without seeing the faces of the lost. We must be so gripped with the personal responsibility of evangelism that it drives us to our knees to call upon the Lord and plead for souls.

Second, time is a "passing opportunity." We not only need to view time as an eternal investment, but as an immediate one as well. We need to remember that each of us will give an account of each day that God gives us. The Apostle Paul writes in Romans 14:12, "So then every one of us shall give account of himself to God." Because of the many opportunities God places in our paths, we're to awake out of our stupor and redeem the time that God allots to each of us.

Do you intend on being a soul winner? When? All we have is now—we're not promised tomorrow. Our lives are like a blank chalkboard, and God allows us to write on it anything we like. As each of us begins the day, may the Lord help us to remember that "time is life" and it is the most precious thing that God gives us apart from salvation.

Jesus is the best example of redeeming the time when He was here on earth. He knew that God had given Him a time limit to fulfill His Father's will. I believe that it was this understanding that filled His heart with an overwhelming urgency for the souls of men who were perishing and needed to be reached with the Gospel. When we very carefully study the life of Jesus, we can see that Jesus could not afford to waste even an hour of His time.

Make the most of your time you have to live here on earth. Wasted time is never regained; Use it wisely, it has great worth.

Help the weak and fallen; make sure we feed the poor. Keep pointing souls to Jesus; that's what we're put there for.

Do the work of the Lord, everyday the whole day through. Redeem the precious time God has given you. Betty Hill

Jesus speaks of the ripe harvest fields in John 4:35. I call this the harvest of present opportunities. He wanted His disciples and Christians today to be consumed with the urgency of reaching souls with the Gospel. "Do you not say, 'There are still four months and then comes the harvest?' Behold, I say to you, lift up your eyes and look at the fields, for they are white already for harvest. Therefore pray the Lord of the harvest to send out laborers into His harvest."

"Jesus did not say, 'go into the field.' He said, 'Therefore pray the Lord of the harvest.' That does not so much mean that the harvest is the world, it means that there are innumerable people who have reached a crisis in their lives, they are 'white already to harvest.' We find them everywhere, not only in foreign countries, but also in neighboring houses, and the way we discern who they are is not by intellect, not by suggestions, but by prayer. Think of the countless crises in people's lives at this time, they are at the parting of the ways."[14]

I received a 2:00 A.M. phone call one night from a neighbor having an asthma attack. Tiffany suffered from frequent asthma attacks the two years that I knew her. It's a very frightful thing when you can't get your breath, and when I met her at the door I could see the fear in her eyes. I could see she was very short of breath and I could hear audible wheezing without using my stethoscope.

I knew that these types of attacks can develop very quickly into a real emergency so I knew I had to work fast. She told me that she couldn't find the medicine for her nebulizer, so I began looking for it and within minutes I found it. I poured the solution into the nebulizer machine and gave it to her to inhale and after about twenty minutes the wheezing subsided and she felt much better.

Tiffany had come to church with me several times, but had never made a profession of faith. However, this time I felt like she was ready to receive Christ, so I asked her very simply if she'd like to have the assurance and joy of Heaven being her eternal home. She started to cry and shared with me that she really wanted to become a Christian, but all her life she had been taught negative things about God, and she didn't know what to believe.

She had been raised in a home where her parents were against attending church, and the only time she heard the name of Jesus was in a swear word. She confided in me that she was very close to her parents, and she didn't know how they would respond if her and her two children accepted Christianity.

She then sincerely asked me how I knew the Bible was the true Word of God. Together we read 2 Peter 1:20, 21,"Knowing this first, that no prophecy of the scripture is of any private interpretation. For the prophecy came not in old time by the will of man: but holy men of God spake as they were moved by the Holy Ghost." Then I took her to 2 Timothy 3:15 where it says, "And that from a child thou hast known the holy scriptures, which are able to make thee wise unto salvation through faith which is in Christ Jesus."

I went on to explain to her that even though the Bible was written by forty different human authors, it was inspired by God and absolutely trustworthy. I said, "The word, 'inspiration,' means 'God-breathed,' and these men were literally 'borne along' by the Holy Spirit as they wrote what God gave them. It means that they were kept from having any error creep into what they wrote."

I shared with her that the Bible has been proven over and over by archaeology and also by fulfilled prophecies. I said to her, "Early in my Christian life I would be overjoyed when the spade of archaeology would prove a fact in the Bible, but the greatest proof in my life is when the Holy Spirit would make Jesus real to my heart. I've seen the transforming power of God work in my life and in lives of others."

I could tell the Holy Spirit was working in her heart as she told me that she wanted that peace and happiness she saw in my life. We read the salvation verses together, and early that morning Tiffany repented of her sins and accepted Christ into her life.

Tiffany was an avid bowler and had received several trophies in her life. I went over to her fireplace, picked up one of her trophies, and said, "Tiffany, just like this trophy, you just became one of the trophies of God's grace." Then, I showed her Ephesians 2:6, 7 where it says that one day in Heaven we will be on display as examples of what God has done. "And hath raised us up together, and made us sit together in heavenly places in Christ Jesus: That in the ages to come he might show the exceeding riches of his grace in his kindness toward us through Christ Jesus."

Tiffany really blessed my heart. I kept in touch with her after I moved to another city, and she shared with me that she was attending a nearby Baptist Church. She had two small children at the time I knew her, and it wasn't long before they trusted Christ as their Savior. She called me one day to tell me that she had been witnessing to her parents and they agreed to visit her church. I sensed the joy in her voice when she told me this and I thanked the Lord for answers to her prayer.

Time is one thing we cannot replace. We need to redeem the time—God only knows how soon our little life may close. Once an hour or a day is gone, we cannot go back and relive it. Consistently, on a daily basis, we should apply Psalm 90:12 to our lives, "So teach us to number our days, that we may apply our hearts unto wisdom."

The famous missionary, Jim Elliot, wrote in his journal, "I seek not a long life, but a full one, like you, Lord Jesus." Life is not a matter of years; it's a matter of what we do with them. What are you doing with the years God has given you?

God has placed a divine call on each of us, and we need to live that calling out in our lives. Queen Esther is a prime example of this. The Lord placed her in a position of influence where she had the chance to save her Jewish people from death. She lived out her divine purpose by rescuing her people. In the divine providence of God, Esther was brought into the kingdom "...For such a time as this" (Esther 4:14).

Now, none of us are given a divine call like Queen Esther, but we all have been given places of influence. You were no accident and where you are right now is no surprise to God. Don't think it strange that God puts you in a particular family, or in a certain job or neighborhood.

God may ask you to do something that you feel hesitant to do. But if He tells you to go, you should go. And if you choose not to, God will get the job done anyway—but you will miss out on the blessing of obeying Him. Just maybe

God has placed you in a certain place, "For such a time as this"—to be an influence for Christ.

"So little time! The harvest will be over, Our reaping done, we reapers taken home. Report our work to Jesus, Lord of harvest, and hope He'll smile and that He'll say, 'Well done!

The harvest white, with reapers few is wasting, and many souls will die and never know the love of Christ, the joy of sins forgiven. Oh, let us weep and love and pray and go!

Today we reap, or miss our golden harvest. Today is given us lost souls to win. Oh, then to save some dear ones from the burning, Today we'll go to bring some sinner in."
Dr. John Rice

Chapter 15

SOWING BESIDE ALL WATERS

"Blessed are ye that sow beside all waters..."
(Isaiah 32:20), or blessed is the soul winner that
tries to reach every soul possible.

We are to sow everywhere, not only in the church, but also in the street, on the job, at school, in the neighborhood—everywhere. We are not only to sow everywhere, but we are to sow all the time. Ecclesiastes 11:4 says, "He that observeth the wind shall not sow;..." In other words, if you wait for all conditions to be favorable, you will not sow.

I love to read about great soul-winners of the past, one of which is Dr. R. A. Torrey. They so encourage my heart to keep on sowing the Word of God even when the conditions are unfavorable. Dr. Torrey was a well-known American evangelist, whose name will be long remembered in regard to thousands of Christian workers in all parts of the world. The following is a story of a dear friend of his:

"An invalid can do personal soul-winning work. I have a friend in New York City who has left a life of wealth and fashion to work among the outcast.

One day she got hold of a poor outcast girl. The girl didn't live much over a year after that lady had led her to

Christ. My friend took her to her home to die. As Delia was dying, she wrote to her friends about receiving Christ, some in Sing Prison, some in the Tombs of New York City—all her friends were among the criminal class. Those who were not behind prison bars she invited to come and see her.

My friend told me, 'There was a constant procession up the stairway to the outcast—women and men who came to see Delia.' Before Delia died, one hundred of the most hopeless men and women in New York she had led to Christ."[15]

This story reminds me of the Pharisees in the New Testament that criticized Jesus for receiving sinners and eating with them. He claimed to be God, and worst of all, He ate and had fellowship with them. It was this socializing with the outcasts of the day that irritated them more than anything.

Perhaps when we want to see Jesus, we'd do well to look where we usually close our eyes and our hearts. He sits in the slums and skid rows of this world. He lives in the hovels and halfway houses. If we are going to be like Jesus, then we will welcome all to our table. He sends us to the unfortunate ones that the world shuns. After all, did not Jesus die for the afflicted and the neglected? Oh, how we need to examine ourselves and ask the Lord to melt our callused and hardened hearts towards the abused and forgotten ones in our world.

I worked three years in a maximum-security prison in Nashville, Tennessee. The Lord gave me many opportunities to give out Bible Correspondence Courses to the most hardened criminals. The following story is about Jason, a forty-year-old man who was considered to be the ringleader of a gang inside the prison. This particular gang is one of the largest and most violent of all the gangs in maximum prisons. It is known to be involved in murders, robberies, and drug dealing, among many other criminal pursuits.

Being the leader, other prisoners would report to Jason of various activities of the prisoners in his gang. If the members didn't adhere to the rules, they would be severely punished, sometimes to the point of death.

Jason was one of my patients in the infirmary part of the prison, a place close by the nursing clinic where they would stay if they had an illness. He was there five months due to a bad foot infection. As I took care of him he would tell me about himself, his home-life, the crime he committed, and how he was coping with prison life. He came from a Christian home where his father was a gospel preacher. He rejected the teaching of the Bible, left home at an early age, and had been sent to jail many times before he was sent to prison.

The Lord provided me with a Christian officer the whole time he was my patient, which made it easy for me to bring in Christian literature. Some officers won't allow the nurses to bring anything in to the patients, but the Lord gave me liberty to distribute literature not only to him, but also to many other prisoners.

During his daily dressing change I had many opportunities to witness to him. I knew that if the Lord would change his life, it would have a direct influence on the other inmates that so needed the Lord in their lives. He gladly accepted the Bible lessons that I offered, and it was a real joy to see him study the Scriptures.

Jason accepted Jesus as his Savior while taking this course and became an avid Bible student until the date of his release from prison. He shared with me that after he was saved he could no longer be involved in the prison gang, and he knew that his life would probably be in danger if he made this decision. But the Lord was with him and gave him protection from the other inmates.

After his foot was healed he was released to the open population of the prison, an area where the prisoners had more freedom to come and go than inmates that were locked up 24/7. During that time the prison gave him permission to hold a weekly Bible class with other inmates, many of whom became Christians.

I often think about him and the tremendous Christian influence he had on other inmates, and not just the inmates, but also on some of the officers. When Christ comes into our lives and makes Himself at home in our hearts, He changes our lives for the good. It says in 2 Corinthians 5:17, "Therefore if any man be in Christ, he is a new creature: old things are passed away; behold, all things are become new."

I know that many inmates get "jailhouse religion," but that's all it is; just religion that will not change their lives. They are not really sorry for the crime they committed, and if given the opportunity, they would do it again. Working there for three years I had the advantage of seeing the real Christians grow in their spiritual life. It isn't always easy living for the Lord in that kind of environment, as some will suffer persecution for their faith from ungodly inmates.

My friend, do you have any idea how valuable one soul is to our Heavenly Father? Every soul is precious in His sight, whether they are on skid row, in a prison cell, or living in a palace. God wants the beggar on the street saved just as much as He wants the millionaire to come to saving faith. Some of the greatest Christians have come from a life of deep sin. Such was the life of John Newton:

"John Newton left England and went to Africa as a slave trader. Eventually he sank so low that he was sold as a slave himself. He lived on crumbs from his owner's table and wild yams, which he dug at night.

His only clothing was a single shirt, which he washed in the ocean. For many months he lived in this base condition.

It does not seem possible for a civilized man to have sunk so low. But the power of Jesus laid hold of him through a missionary. He became a sea captain; later he became a minister. He wrote many hymns sung the world around; the most famous is *Amazing Grace*."[16]

After his conversion, he became known as the "sailor preacher" of London and God used him to bring thousands to a saving faith in the Lord Jesus. In the church of London of which he was pastor, there is still an epitaph John Newton wrote for himself. It reads:

"Sacred to the memory of John Newton, once a libertine and blasphemer and slave of slaves in Africa, but renewed, purified, pardoned and appointed to preach that Gospel which he labored to destroy."

We, as believers, have the greatest privilege in the world. Telling people how to be saved is the greatest thing you can do for them. If your friend had cancer and you knew the cure, wouldn't it be criminal to withhold that information from him? We have the cure for sin and its death sentence, and we fall short of what God has called us to do if we fail to give out the gospel.

Chapter 16

HERE COMES THE BRIDE

"The thing proceedeth from the Lord."
"A marriage is likely to be comfortable when it appears
to proceed from the Lord."
John Wesley

There are many exciting stories in the Bible, one of which is found in Genesis 24 where we have the delightful story of the trusted servant of Abraham getting a bride for Isaac.

Here we see Abraham and his son, Isaac, living in the land of Canaan. Abraham was very concerned that Isaac should not marry one of the Canaanite women, but one of his kindred. Abraham and his servant, Eliezer, agreed that God must provide the right woman for Isaac.

God's leading can be seen all through this chapter, and it was God that controlled all the circumstances. Eliezer was told to go into a far country of Mesopotamia, unto the city of Nahor. The servant called upon the Lord to give him wisdom and good success in this endeavor. He was led to the house of his master's brethren, those of which were not idolaters, but worshippers of the true God.

How is Eliezer to know the right girl that God has selected? He knew that she had to be a very special girl, someone that was humble and industrious, very courteous and hospitable to strangers.

His prayer of faith was answered when he arrived in the city and he and his camels rested beside a well at the time when the women of the city came to draw water. He decides to make a serious test—he will ask the girl for a drink of water and then she must voluntarily offer to draw water for all his ten camels. They would be very thirsty as they had been on a long journey of 450 miles across desert country.

As he is resting, he lifts up his eyes and sees a beautiful girl named Rebekah drawing water from the well. She exactly fulfills all the proposed conditions—she offers to draw water for Eliezer and also for all his camels. One camel would take at least a half of a barrel of water at one time, so it must have taken her a long time to draw water for his ten camels.

Upon talking with this woman, he finds out to his great satisfaction that she was a relative of his master, and that her family would give him and his animals lodging.

I want to point out a principle that we can learn from this story. The believer that walks in the way of the Lord may find that God guides all his steps. He arranges all the incidents and orchestrates the people behind the scenes to get you to your divine destiny.

If God would guide this trusted servant of Abraham, then He will guide any of His children who rely upon Him and walk in His way. I love Genesis 24:27, "...I being in the way, the Lord led me to the house of my master's brethren." We can apply this to our lives. We need to be always "in the way" of people that need to know about our wonderful Savior.

Eliezer is very welcomed to the home of Rebekah. Right away he states his reason for coming, and this is the response from her parents in Genesis 24:50, "…. the thing proceedeth from the Lord…behold, Rebekah is before thee, take her, and go, and let her be thy master's son's wife, as the Lord hath spoken." So Eliezer takes Rebekah and her servants, and they start on their journey.

I've often wondered what thoughts were racing through both their minds before they actually met. I just imagine Isaac would wonder if she was beautiful and would she love him. I wonder if he was thinking about the multitude of descendants that would be "As the dust of the earth and as the stars of the sky," which would come from him and through this woman coming to be his bride.

Through Rebekah's long journey she had pictured the man she had never seen. Would he be handsome, strong and kind to her? Would they have many children? Would she be beautiful to him? Would she ever see her parents again?

It was evening when Rebekah saw Isaac for the first time. And, what did she find him doing? He was alone, meditating and conversing with the Lord in the open field as he waited for his future bride. How this should speak to our hearts today. People today cannot stand to be in solitude and silence is almost unbearable to them.

When we are alone, meditating on the things of God should be our delight, but the noise of the world crowds this out in the lives of many Christians. We always have to have the television or the radio on—anything to make a noise. How sad it is when Christians desire to feed on the junk of this world instead of communing with their God.

My God and I go in the field together, We walk and talk as good friends should and do; We clasp our hands, our voices ring with laughter, My God and I walk thru the meadow's hue.

My God and I will go for aye together, We'll walk and talk and just as good friends do; This earth will pass, and with it common trifles—But God and I will go unendingly.
I. B. Sergei

Take note of what Rebekah did when she saw her beloved—she behaved very becomingly. The Bible says she covered her face with a veil, which denotes humility, modesty and subjection.

The Bible says in Ephesians 5:22, "Wives, submit yourselves unto your own husbands, as unto the Lord." Again, in I Timothy 2:9 we're reminded that they should "...adorn themselves in modest apparel..." How modern-day marriages could learn from the example portrayed in this story.

Ephesians 5:25 instructs the husbands to love and cherish their wives. "Husbands, love your wives, even as Christ also loved the church, and gave himself for it." They are to lead their wives in a loving way, as Christ leads His people in a loving manner.

The wedding took place right away. "And Isaac brought her into his mother Sarah's tent, and took Rebekah, and she became his wife; and he loved her: and Isaac was comforted after his mother's death" (Genesis 24:67). Oh, what a joy this bride was to the hungry heart of Isaac.

I want to point out some startling illustrations in this beautiful story. First of all, Isaac is a type of Christ. The trusted servant typifies the Holy Spirit in going out to a far country to find a bride for Isaac, just like He is today assembling that blessed group of people that will be the heavenly Bride of Jesus.

Rebekah, symbolizing the Bride of Christ, went on a long journey to meet her beloved and loved Isaac long before she saw him. The Bride of Christ is taught to love the yet unseen Bridegroom. "We love Him because He first loved us." (I John 4:19).

The Bride of Christ is presently on a long journey to meet her Bridegroom, and some glorious day at the Rapture the bride will see His blessed face and be with Him forever. But in the meanwhile, what should be the Bride's true attitude? It is to be delighting in His will; to be devoted to all

His interests; to long for His coming and the joys of our heavenly home.

The Bible says that we typify that trusted servant of Abraham as we go forth taking the gospel to all nations. What an awesome privilege and responsibility we have in winning the lost to the Savior, and how fervent and bold we should be in our witness for the Lord.

I remember working with a young nurse that had just become a new bride. Cheryl and her husband attended a large prestigious church in town, but she shared with me that something was missing in their marriage. She knew I was a Christian, so she began to ask me questions about the Bible and the differences between the denominations.

I could tell she was searching for the truth, so after work I took her out for coffee and I had the blessed privilege of sharing with her how I became a Christian. As I showed her from my New Testament how she could be saved, she told me that she had never heard a clear presentation of the gospel. She had been taught that going through the motions of baptism, partaking of communion, and confirmation were enough to take her to Heaven.

Because I knew that she was trusting in church ordinances to save her, I showed her I Peter 1:18, 19 where it says that we can only be redeemed by putting our faith in the precious blood of Christ. "Forasmuch as ye know that ye were not redeemed with corruptible things, as silver and gold, from your vain conversation received by tradition from your fathers; But with the precious blood of Christ, as of a lamb without blemish and without spot."

I gave her a special "faith gospel" pamphlet that explained what it means to trust Christ: Faith means, *FORSAKING ALL I TRUST HIM*. That day, Cheryl pressed the delete button and deleted all the church's ordinances she had been trusting in to save her, and put her trust only in the precious blood of

Jesus for salvation. Instantly, she became part of the glorious Bride of Christ.

Six months after Cheryl's conversion, her husband was transferred to a job in another state. She wrote me and said that they were going to a small, non-denominational church where her husband had made a profession of faith. It was encouraging to know that they were growing in their Christian walk with the Lord.

I find it amazing how many people rely on the ordinances of the church for salvation. Let me explain what I told Cheryl: Baptism does not save anyone. It shows our identification with Christ in His death, burial, and resurrection. As we are immersed under the water, this pictures the death and burial of the old nature before we were saved. Coming up out of the water, it pictures the resurrection of a new life to be lived for the Lord Jesus.

Baptism shows to the world what has taken place in our hearts. Just like the Lord's Supper, baptism has no saving power—they are pictures of what the Lord Jesus has done for us. They are beautiful pictures of spiritual truth.

This ordinance is for believers only and is not an option, but a command to follow after conversion. We must be saved before baptism takes place and have a clear understanding of what it is. Baptism is the first step of obedience for the new believer, and if we are truly saved and love the Lord, then, we will not hesitate to follow our Lord's command.

Chapter 17

PRICELESS TREASURES

Sometimes beautiful treasures are often contained in most unlikely packages. We need to see every person as our Heavenly Father sees them—valuable, dearly loved and precious.

As believers, we have a priceless treasure that this world can never take from us—And what is this treasure? It is the glorious gospel. "But we have this treasure in earthen vessels..." (2 Corinthians 4:7). The Apostle Paul is saying that we carry this incredible treasure in our little, old earthen bodies.

But did you know that God has deposited many other treasures on the inside of you? As we submit ourselves to the Lord on a daily basis, we discover the treasures within—joy, mercy, boldness in witnessing, humility, kindness, patience, love, peace, spiritual wisdom and revelation, and the list goes on.

If we had beautiful, expensive jewelry, we would not carelessly throw it around. No, we would guard and protect it. And there is something else we would do—we would love to display it in some fashion.

In the same way we would display our earthly valuables, we should draw out those treasures that lie on the inside of us and put them on display to a lost world. When a lost person sees us showing them love and mercy, they will want what we have. Christians should be the most loving and kind people in the world; always ready to go the extra mile to do an act of kindness to a needy individual.

I have found in my nursing profession that when I display those treasures to an unsaved patient, then those blessings boomerang back to me and I see His hand of blessing in every area of my life. In other words, God will honor us if we put His agenda ahead of ours.

"The old Bible lay on a bargain table amidst hundreds of tattered books. Many people picked it up and thumbed through its faded pages. It wasn't in very good shape—certainly not worth two pounds, so it was cast aside.

But then a man picked up the Bible and stifled a shout. He rushed to the counter and paid the paltry sum for the old book. It was an original Gutenberg, estimated to be worth over one million dollars. I wonder who turned it over to the 'last chance' booksellers? How many times did the old Bible change hands before its redemption? Someone cast it aside, unaware of its value."[17]

Besides all the treasures that are deposited on the inside of us, there is another treasure that we so often will treat like the old Bible—people. We are His most precious creation, created in the image of God. We are God's special handiwork or masterpiece. Each of us is uniquely made with different gifts and talents, and not one of us should be over-looked. We often cast aside those that we feel are insignificant, but remember that they are priceless to our Heavenly Father.

I often think of the Apostle Peter, poor, un-educated, and considered to be a nobody when Jesus called him to follow Him. Jesus didn't look at his tattered clothes and his occupation as a fisherman. No, He looked at the inner man and saw a soul of great value. And after Peter was filled with the Holy Spirit, He became one of the leaders of the early church, and what a giant of the faith he became. Isn't it wonderful that God chooses unexceptional people like Peter, and you and me, to build His kingdom?

Look closely at a divine appointment that Jesus had with the Samaritan woman in John 4:1-39. Meeting with this woman was no accident on the part of Jesus. Little is known about this woman and what we do know is not good. She was very immoral and considered to be an outcast to the Jews and to her own people. She was very popular with the men of the village who used her for their own physical pleasure and then tossed her aside like a broken doll.

But when Jesus saw her, He loved her—just as she was. He looked at this sinful woman through eyes of compassion and saw a priceless treasure. He recognized her worth. Because of the change that Jesus made in her life, she became a missionary to her own people, and the Bible says that many Samaritans believed on Jesus through her testimony.

I love what Dr. David Jeremiah writes about these priceless people that the world so despises: "God the Father and God the Son covenanted together to bless you regardless of your worth in the eyes of the world. In God's eyes, the life of His Son is the measure of your true worth."

I admire my sister that patiently corrects Bible Correspondence lessons that she sends to prison inmates all over the United States. Week after week she goes over their lessons, corrects them and prays for each one. She will probably never meet them on this earth, but one day in Heaven she'll see the results of her labor. Why does she patiently correct their lessons? Because she looks beyond the crime they committed and sees seeds of greatness in each one.

When I worked in the Virgin Islands I took care of a patient that was dying of complications from HIV. She had lived in Haiti where there is a high incidence of this disease, and she had moved back to St. Thomas to be with what little family she had. I could tell she was fearful and very lonely, as she didn't have many friends or family that came to see her.

I got to know her fairly well the four weeks I took care of her before she died. I remember how her beautiful dark eyes would fill with tears as she shared with me her home life and the poor conditions where she had lived. She told me how her baby son died at the age of two, and how painful it was for her to lose him.

I could tell that at one time she had been an attractive lady with her long, wavy dark hair and beautiful smile. There were still traces of that beauty, but that beauty was fast fading with each passing day. I could tell that her days were numbered and I prayed I could win her to the Lord.

My prayers were answered. One day when it was fairly quiet, I sat beside her, took her hand in mine, and simply told her how Jesus loved her and wanted to save her. That day she repented of her sins and accepted Jesus into her life. She said, "I have heard stories of Jesus before, but no one had ever told me that He wanted to be my personal Savior."

As she knew she was slowly dying, she asked me about Heaven and what it was like, so I tried to describe this magnificent city of shimmering beauty. I took her to the book of Revelation and read chapters 20 and 21 to her, and I never will forget how large her eyes would get when I shared these spiritual truths with her. I went on to say, "Even though Heaven is a place of dazzling beauty, it cannot be compared to the beauty and the glory of our Lord Jesus."

She especially loved Revelation 21:4 where it says, "God will wipe away every tear from their eyes; there shall be no more death, nor sorrow, nor crying...there shall be no more pain; for the former things have passed away." She then made the comment, "I just can't imagine life without tears and pain."

One day when I was giving her medication, she was watching a TV show where there was an emotional scene of a young man dying. She looked up and asked, "Will it be painful when it comes time for me to die?" I read to her I Corinthians 15:54, 55, "...Death is swallowed up in victory. O death, where is thy sting? O grave, where is thy victory?" I told her, "Christ took away the painful sting of death for the believer when He died on the cross and rose again."

I quoted her that precious promise in 2 Corinthians 5:8 where it says, "We are confident, I say, and willing rather to be absent from the body, and to be present with the Lord." I went on to tell her, "Death for the Christian is not oblivion or darkness, but it's entering a bright new day of perfect and glorious life."

I told her, "Crissa, when it comes time for you to die, you will gently close your eyes and awaken in God's presence. When you take that last breath, the angels of God will carry you straight to Heaven where you will be with your Savior and your little one for eternity." I sat down beside her and held her hand until she fell asleep. Just before the pain medication took effect, she whispered, "Thank you." It brought tears to my eyes, and I thanked the dear Lord Jesus that she would be soon be free of pain forever.

I wasn't on duty when she passed into the everlasting arms of her Heavenly Father, but I rejoice that I had the chance to give her the glorious gospel and to know that she gladly accepted it. I know I'll see her in Heaven someday. Oh, how we need to *Rescue the perishing and care for the dying!*

In the eyes of the world, this poor woman would not have been of much value, but she was a priceless treasure in the eyes of God. We need to show the same compassion and love that Jesus demonstrated to the poor and the social outcasts when He was here on earth. We need to adhere to the words in Jude 22, 23. "And of some have compassion, making a difference, and others save with fear, pulling them out of the fire; hating even the garment spotted by the flesh."

"Are you lonely? Then seek to find someone more sorrowful; and then, if only you can but point him to that Living One whose loving touch can bind the broken heart. A blessed work is done, which through Eternity will last, and you will find His perfect peace and joy possess your mind and soul."
Paul Lormar

"One day a man in Boston had in his Sunday School class a boy fresh from the country. This dull boy knew almost nothing about the Bible. He didn't even know where to look to find the Gospel of John. He was very much put out because the other boys were bright boys and knew their Bibles, while he was just a green country boy.

But that Sunday school teacher had a heart full of love to Christ and perishing souls. One day he went down into the boot shop where that boy worked and asked him, 'Would you like to be a Christian?' The boy had never been approached that way before. Nobody had ever spoken to him about his soul. He said, 'Yes, I would like to be a Christian.'

And that teacher explained what it meant to be a Christian, and then said, 'Let us pray.' They knelt down in the back of that boot shop, and the boy became a Christian. That boy was Dwight L. Moody, who later became one of America's most famous evangelists."[18]

Teacher, there may be children in your class that may be slow learners, maybe even mentally challenged. And, they may come from a bad environment, but God sees them as valuable. Seeds of greatness are often buried in a person that we think will never amount to anything. Who knows what that poor little boy or girl may become? We need to remember where each of us have come from, and that we were all lost in our sin when Jesus saw something of value in us.

"We are the tangible manifestation of the compassionate heart of our Father. You and I are the expression of God's love on this earth." Florence Littauer

Chapter 18

TO TRINIDAD FOR ONE SOUL

*When you open your heart to the Lord,
He will open your eyes to the lost around you.*

While working in St. Thomas, the Lord gave me the opportunity to help in a small Baptist Church on the Island of St. John. I would take a ferry boat from St. Thomas to St. John every Sunday, and ferry back after the evening service I cannot begin to describe the beautiful scenery between the two islands.

Pastor Emmanuel Jaggernauth and his lovely wife, Merle, were a delightful couple, and I so enjoyed their fellowship. While I was there Merle and I flew to Trinidad to visit her father and step-mother.

**Pastor Emmanuel and Merle Jaggernauth,
St. John, The Virgin Islands**

As we flew over several islands I thought my heart would burst with the beautiful scenery we passed. I kept meditating on Psalm 19:1 where it says, "The heavens declare the glory of God, and the firmament showeth his handiwork." We certainly have a majestic Creator and our hearts should praise Him daily for His wonderful works.

We had one lay-over on the way to Trinidad, and that stop was the lovely Island of Antigua. Friends of Merle met us at the airport and we had a great time of relaxation and fellowship. They took us to a beautiful beachfront and treated us to a delicious lunch of a tasty seafood salad, homemade bread, lemonade, and a light chocolate mousse. God is so good to each one of us—even in the little things of life He showers His blessings upon us. Praise His wonderful Name!

Upon arriving in Trinidad, a minister and his wife met us and drove us around the island, pointing out several places of interest. Trinidad has a beautiful coastline and is noted for their fantastic beaches. The water is crystal clear and swimming with all kinds of diverse marine life. People from all over the world come here and to the sister island of Tobago just to snorkel and deep-sea dive.

We enjoyed the wonderful hospitality of Merle's parents. They took us to a certain high mountain where we could look down and see Venezuela. Trinidad lies just seven miles off the northeastern coast of Venezuela. I didn't realize they were so close together, and as I gazed at the beauty of this unique country, I couldn't help but think of the thousands of lost people living in that land. I knew that Roman Catholicism is the dominant religion in that country with very few Christians.

Hanatia, (Merle's stepmother), Merle Jaggernauth and her father, in The Island of Trinidad

While there are many beautiful, natural attractions in Trinidad, there are also many places where my heart ached for the people. Many of the people are poor and live in crowded, filthy shacks. The market places were very dirty and unkempt, and crime was very prevalent in these areas.

One particular scene will be forever embedded on my mind. We stopped and watched a Hindu funeral that was held in an outdoor wooded area. The deceased had been wrapped in a blanket and the skull had been crushed so as to release the soul of the departed. The body was then lifted onto a flat board and shoved into the pyre. Then a member of the family would light the pyre.

While the deceased was being cremated some of the people would be chanting as they marched around the pyre. Others could be heard wailing and crying for miles around. This whole scene was very eerie to me and I could just feel the presence of evil.

A Hindu Funeral Pyre

As I solemnly watched this ordeal my thoughts went back to the various Christian burials that I've attended. Yes, we mourn for our precious loved ones, but not as those who have no hope. What a difference that makes. The Bible says in 2 Corinthians 5:8 "...absent from the body, present with the Lord." Believers that die will be in complete fellowship with the Lord while they await the eventual resurrection of their bodies. Another beloved verse is found in Psalm 116:15, "Precious in the sight of the Lord is the death of His saints."

Loss and death are a part of life, but Christians can face them, knowing that we'll never say goodbye for the last time. For the unsaved person, death is a fearful prospect, a black unknown. For the believer, death means an entrance into the presence of our Heavenly Father. We can comfort one another with the hope of the resurrection and a future reunion.

These precious Hindu people have no hope beyond the grave and will never see their family members again. Believers in the Lord Jesus should be the most thankful people on earth as they have the truth of the living God, and our hearts should ache for people that worship false gods.

Most forms of Hinduism are henotheistic. They recognize other gods as facets, manifestations of that supreme god. Many rural Hindus worship their own village goddess. She is believed to rule over fertility and disease, thus over life and death. They also believe in the transfer of one's soul after death into another body. This produces a continuing cycle of birth, life, death and rebirth through their many lifetimes.

The day before we left, Merle's stepmother, Hanatia, and I were engaged in a conversation comparing the different religions of the world, mainly Hinduism and Christianity. Merle had shared with me that her father and stepmother were not saved before our trip, and I could tell by our conversation that she was very intelligent with worldly wisdom, but did not possess joy or peace in her heart that only our Lord can give. Her father attended the Church of Christ, and believed that water baptism plus faith in God would save him.

During our talk, I silently prayed that the conversation would be focused on salvation. Many times when we talk to people, Satan will slyly move the conversation into rabbit trails that won't profit anything, so we should always strive to steer the conversation around the person of the Lord Jesus.

As we continued to talk she said, "All religions worship the same god—they just have different ways of worshipping and eventually all those that sincerely seek this Supreme Being will end up in Heaven." I reminded her of the look of hopelessness and despair on the faces of those at the funeral. Then I said, "Would you really want to believe and put your faith in the god they worship? The god they worship is dead and they have no hope in this world and in eternity."

Hanatia then commented, "I've always believed that as long as we're sincere in our religion, then, that sincerity will save us." I said, "Sincerity is important, but it's not an adequate substitute for knowing the truth of God's Word. Many people are in Hell today because they sincerely believed in a false religion."

I could tell by her attitude and our conversation that she was seeking the truth. She told me that she sincerely wanted to know what was right and had gone to several different churches, but had become so confused that she had given up.

As I silently prayed for God to give me wisdom, I said, "Let's compare the Bible's way of salvation with those of other religions. In the Hindu religion, they believe they have to do agonizing acts to receive God's favor. Muslims involve themselves in a strict habit of fasting and prayer to earn God's approval. Any world religion revolves around a belief of "good works" to satisfy a Holy God. The Bible offers us a salvation not by our works, but by grace through faith."

I opened my Bible and we read together John 14:6 where it says that Jesus is the only door to Heaven. I said, "Jesus didn't say 'I am a way.' He said He is 'The Way." Then, I showed her John 6:68 where it says, "Then Simon Peter answered him, Lord, to whom shall we go? Thou hast the words of eternal life."

I had her read I Timothy 2:5, "For there is one God, and one mediator between God and men, the man Christ Jesus. Who gave himself a ransom for all." I made the comment, "Christ is our Savior, our Redeemer, our Mediator who brings God and man together. Jesus died for us. He will bring you right through to God if you will turn to Him." Then, we read together that tremendous verse in Acts 4:12, "Neither is there salvation in any other; for there is none other name under heaven given among men, whereby we must be saved."

I went on to explain to her that religion without Christ will never satisfy the seeking heart. I said, "Of the many world religions, only one claims that its founder returned from the grave. The resurrection of Jesus Christ is the very cornerstone of Christianity, and the Bible records the eyewitness accounts. If you go to Buddha's tomb, he'll be there. But if you go to the tomb of Jesus, you'll find it empty. The Christian's hope is alive today because of the empty tomb."

I knew that Merle and her family had prayed for years for this dear lady's salvation and had frequently planted the seed in her heart. So as I silently watered the seed by prayer, I began to notice a softening about her, and I could tell the Holy Spirit was working in her heart.

I said, "Hanatia, only Jesus, called the Living Water, can satisfy your thirsty soul. In the book of the Revelation, He is called the 'Water of Life.' You've tasted of the world's religions, and they didn't satisfy you. Wouldn't you right now like to taste of this Living Water and give God a chance in your life? Psalm 34:8 says, "O taste and see that the Lord is good." That night the Lord have me the privilege of leading this precious lady to the Lord.

Always remember that the Lord receives all the praise and glory when a soul is won. Someone plants the seed, another waters, and another one reaps; but it is God who gives the increase. God is simply giving us the blessed privilege of participating in the process. John 4:36 tells us, "And he that reapeth receiveth wages, and gathereth fruit unto life eternal: that both he that soweth and he that reapeth may rejoice together."

After giving her heart to the Lord, she said to me, "How can the Lord use me at my age?" I replied, "God can use people at any age—all they need to be is a willing vessel." I shared with her the story of Philip, the new convert in John 1:45. I said, "As soon as he found Jesus, he readily found his friend, Nathanael, and reported to him that he found the Messiah. We need to share the gospel with our friends and neighbors, and give our testimony of what Jesus did for us and what He's willing to do in their lives."

Before we left the next morning, I left her with a little booklet on how to grow as a Christian. I explained to her that it is so vital that she start growing in the faith, as Satan will work hard on her to discourage her in every way possible. Merle knew a minister of a small Baptist Church near where she lived, so she called him to follow up with her.

This lady really blessed my heart. One month after our visit, Merle told me that her stepmother had been witnessing to her husband, and praying for his salvation.

"You can instruct everyone whom you lead to Christ to go out and be a soul winner. After you get hold of him, send him out, when converted, to lead another; and he bringing one, and that one bringing in another." Dr. R. A. Torrey

Chapter 19

GOD USES JUST ORDINARY PEOPLE

*"These people intrigue me because they enshrine
a great truth: God takes delight in nobodies,
invests them with beauty and greatness, and uses them
to touch the world with grace and truth."*
David Roper

What kind of person does God look for to use for His glory? And what qualifies a person to be selected by God to be His instrument in bringing lost souls into God's kingdom? What about people whom the world would classify as just ordinary? Is there a place for someone like that? I find all through Scripture that God seems to go out of His way to use people whom you'd never imagine He would.

Paul tells us in I Corinthians 1:27, 29 why God does this. "But God hath chosen the foolish things of the world to confound the wise; and God hath chosen the weak things of the world to confound the things which are mighty...That no flesh should glory in his presence."

God delights in doing extraordinary things through ordinary people, and today He works the same way. Most of us are quite ordinary. We love to read inspiring biographies of great Christians who the Lord has saved out of deep sin, but few people have lived a life of such drama.

I appreciate those people that transmit the love of Jesus in their every day secular jobs. You will never see their names in the newspaper columns or on TV, but you can be sure of one thing—Their Heavenly Father is watching and keeps a record of their service for Him. Always remember He is always watching to see if we'll be faithful in our present circumstances.

A humble Sunday School teacher that is faithful every week or a missionary working with a remote heathen tribe in the most isolated place is no less loved by our Lord than the greatest preacher, and will in no way lose their reward. Jesus said in Luke 16 that our Lord finds pleasure in those servants who are "faithful over a few things."

Many Christians think that they can't be used of God because of lack of talent, personal charm, or training, but be encouraged that Jesus loves you just as you are and whoever you are. He loves you as much as the greatest evangelist. I'm so thankful that God doesn't call us because we are particularly gifted or talented. If that were so, I would have never been called. He delights in using us because we choose to be obedient to Him. I love the old saying. "He doesn't call the qualified—He qualifies the called."

Let me share a true story I read of how God used just an ordinary man to win souls. This story really blessed my heart and so encouraged me to keep on witnessing for my Lord.

"Several times, in a western city, I have had the privilege of meeting a dear Christian brother who has been a helpless invalid for over fifteen years. He loves the house of God, and is brought to the services on a stretcher. There he lies and listens—flat, rigid, arms and legs paralyzed, hands and feet twisted, both eyes now blind, but a brightness on his face that reminds one of a pleasant sunrise. One day a middle-aged lady told me that she had formerly been his nurse. She had not wanted to look after such a helpless case, but now she could never thank God enough that she had been given the privilege, for it was her dear invalid who had brought her to Christ. About the same time I learned that one hundred and sixty other persons had been converted to Christ through him, some by letter, some by interview, some by telephone. Again and again people call him by phone on spiritual matters. He 'rejoices evermore' and is 'always abounding in the work of the Lord.' He has transformed his very helplessness into a vehicle of service for Christ"[19]

While working the night shift on the Medical-Surgical Unit I had the privilege of taking care of an eighteen year old teen-ager that was dying of a rare bone cancer, and was given about six months to live. Every so often Ron had to be admitted to the hospital for blood transfusions and each time he was admitted I was assigned to him as his nurse.

As I remember him, he was a very nice, well-mannered boy that would always try to make the workload easier for the nurses. I marveled at his beautiful attitude and it made me wonder if he was a Christian. One night was especially quiet so I spent extra time visiting with him. In our conversation he asked me, "Why did you choose the nursing profession?"

I replied, "I enjoy helping people, but the main reason I became a nurse was because it's a profession where you have many opportunities to share the love of Jesus with your patients."

He asked me then where I went to church. I said, "I go to a Baptist Church, but even though church is very important in the believers' life, the most important thing is having a personal relationship with the Lord Jesus."

"I don't know what you mean by that," he answered back. So, I had the blessed privilege of telling him how to know Jesus in a personal way. He didn't make a decision at that time, but I could tell there was a real desire to know more about spiritual things.

Before I left that day he asked me if I would leave my New Testament with him to read. I usually don't leave my

Bible with anyone since it's a very special Soul Winning New Testament that I didn't want to lose, but I made an exception in his case and was so glad that I did. He asked me where he should start reading, so I told him the Gospel of John was a good place to start.

When I came back to work two days later he had read all four Gospels and part of the book of Romans. He told me, "This is all so new to me. I have never owned a Bible and have never been to church in my life. The only time I've heard about Jesus is in a swear word." He had all kinds of questions and I tried to answer them as best I could. He was a very serious person, and I could tell by his questions that he was concerned about life after death.

Before that week was over, God gave me the opportunity to show this teen-ager how to be born-again. He repented of his sins and asked Jesus to be his personal Savior. I rejoice that some day I will see him in Heaven as one of the trophies of God's grace.

Every time I think of him I just thank the Lord so much that He gave me a small part in his salvation. I'm reminded of the verses in 2 Corinthians 2:15, 16 "For we are unto God a sweet savor of Christ, in them that are saved, and in them that perish: To the one we are the savor of death unto death; and to the other the savor of life unto life." These are pretty serious words from Jesus and I just marvel that He gives us such an awesome privilege and responsibility.

Some time later he died at home with his mother at his side. I had known Barbara as she worked as a respiratory therapist at the same hospital where I worked. I saw her about a week after the funeral and offered my condolences. I said, "Barbara, I'd like to share something special with you. "The last time I took care of Ron, He became a Christian by putting his trust in the Lord Jesus to save him."

But she scoffed at what I told her and replied, "Well, I'm glad you were so good to him, but I don't believe there is a

God after seeing my son suffer so much." I thought again of the above verse, "To the one we are the savor of death unto death." How sad to have a mother like that. Even though she was angry with God, she did take the gospel tract I offered her. I can only pray that some day she will give her heart to the Lord.

We must constantly keep in mind that the gospel is not good news only, but it is a judgment as well to those that hear it and reject it. The message of salvation is indeed good news to the one who gladly receives it, but to those that obey not the gospel, it carries a severe warning.

Do you feel that your testimony is just too "ordinary" to share with others? I felt that way for a long time because I was saved as a child—there was no drama in my life before conversion. But just remember that no matter how common our testimony may sound compared to someone else's, the Lord will use it.

What the Lord has done for any of us is just as extraordinary as what He did for the murderer, drug dealer, or the prostitute. Isaiah 55:11 reminds us, "So shall my word be that goeth forth out of my mouth: it shall not return unto me void, but it shall accomplish that which I please, and it shall prosper in the thing whereto I sent it."

The ordinary life can be lived very beautifully if we allow the Lord to use us in every aspect of our lives. There are godly men and women that shine in the limelight, but this world is in dire need of Christians that will live the ordinary life in a really out-of-the-ordinary way.

We should not want elaborate forms of service, but instead plead for the Lord to give us a pure and humble spirit, and be prepared for opportunities that He may give us. You have no idea how God will take your ordinary testimony and use it for His honor and glory. I like what D.L. Moody said, "We may easily be too big for God to use, but never too small."

My friend, "Do you feel too small for God to use you?" Well, take heart, because I want to tell a delightful story in the Bible where a little maid was used in a very mighty way to bring an arrogant Syrian commander to the Lord. This insignificant maid, who was taken captive in a foreign land, is a wonderful example in soul winning. This great story shows, too, of the wonderful ways that our God reaches men of heathen minds and backgrounds.

The great notable Naaman in the book of 2 Kings 5 had honor and power, but he had leprosy, one of the most appalling diseases in the world. The Bible doesn't say what stage his leprosy was, but we know it was a terminal illness that would leave his body in a very shocking state of gross ugliness, not to mention the state of loneliness and isolation he would have to suffer.

Unbeknown to Naaman, God had a wonderful plan for his life, and it all started with a Jewish slave girl that loved the true and living God. Naaman and his family were of heathen descent and worshipped idols. He was a rough man, but I'm sure underneath his hardened exterior he was a desperate man, crying out for help. He had called on his gods for healing to no avail.

Seeing the desperate condition of her master, the maiden said to Naaman's wife in 2 Kings 5:3, "If only my master would see the prophet who is in Samaria! He would cure him of his leprosy." His wife reported this to Naaman, and immediately he believed her and sought permission from the king to visit Elisha, the prophet.

But a very strange thing happened. Instead of Elisha coming to Naaman and healing him, he sent a messenger to him with this announcement in 2 Kings 5:10, "Go, wash in Jordan, seven times, and thy flesh shall come again to thee, and thou shalt be clean." But Naaman was furious with Elisha, thinking he should at least come to him and wave his hand over the leprosy, and call upon the name of the Lord.

After all, Naaman was a very important man in Syria—how dare anyone treat him in this way! So, in his prideful rage, he turned away from the word of God—unchanged.

We read where Naaman thought at least Elisha should have picked the clean waters of Damascus rather than the murky waters of the Jordan River that looked like liquid mud. But God was looking at his prideful heart, and He knew what it would take to bring this arrogant man to repentance.

Sometimes God has to lay us low and bring us through the "muddy Jordan River" before we see our need of salvation. Pride is the root of all sins—and this sin of pride, passed on from Lucifer to Adam and Eve in the Garden, is what Satan uses to blind us from the truth.

The Bible says that after his servants reasoned with him; he yielded and obeyed God's Word. And to his surprise and joy, "his flesh came again, like unto the flesh of a little child" (verse 14). And his response to God was one of faith and worship. Look at verse 15, "Behold, now I know that there is no God in all the earth, but in Israel." After he was saved, his pride and arrogance left him. He came in humility, and left with a blessing. Always remember that promised blessings come after obedience.

Just as Naaman was urged to "Wash and be clean," so God urges all people to "Believe and be saved"—"Repent and be pardoned." The methods laid out here in Scripture for the healing of the leprosy of sin are so plain to see that we are utterly inexcusable if we pass them by.

I get so encouraged every time I think of this little maid. She had every reason to hate her master as he had held her a captive slave, away from her home and country. But she grew to love Naaman and his wife. This little girl was not only able to bring healing to her master, but was responsible for his conversion.

God is showing us here that the weakest may win the strongest. An uneducated Wesleyan teacher won Charles

Spurgeon, the prince of preachers, to the Lord. Dwight L. Moody was won by a humble Sunday school teacher. If a Christian has love in his heart and depends on the power of the Holy Spirit, there is no limit on how he can be used of God.

My friend, you may feel unimportant and unknown in this world, but you can do great things for God—all it takes is a heart full of love and devotion to our Lord. God is looking for unexpected and ordinary people to use for His glory. Are you willing to be one of them?

Chapter 20

BECOME A PERSON OF PASSION

We need to pray that God's passionate heart can be released through us. His very heartbeat is people.

Are you living a life that taps into your passion and purpose? All of us need to discover what we're passionate about. We do this so we can live life with a greater sense of significance. Have you ever been around passionless people? They change nothing.

The Apostle Paul comes to my mind when I think of a person with passion. Paul's passion in life was mainly driven by concern for the eternal destiny of others. I used to think of him as a very stern, cleric-type person, but after studying his character I've seen a different side to him.

Romans 9:2, 3 tells us that he had a very passionate concern for his own Jewish brethren that they would be saved and come to the knowledge of the truth. "For I could wish that myself were accursed from Christ for my brethren…" In other words, he was willing to go to Hell if that would save his people from perishing. That, my friend, is passionate love.

I find Jesus weeping at the tomb of Lazarus. How He must have loved him. And then, I see him weeping with strong crying and tears in the Garden of Gethsemane. Our

God is a God of passion. God is so passionately in love with people that when you cry for those you love, you're really helping Him cry.

One of my favorite verses in soul winning is found in Psalm 126:6, "He that goeth forth and weepeth, bearing precious seed, shall doubtless come again with rejoicing, bringing his sheaves with him." Here, tears are seen as compassionate caring. I like this verse because God attaches a wonderful promise to it—but it's contingent on our obedience.

This verse presents a wonderful outline on how to have God's power and how to experience results in soul winning. Here is the promise that one who goes after sinners, one who has concern and a broken heart, and one who uses the precious seed of the gospel, shall undoubting lead some people to salvation. We're not promised that everyone will be saved when we witness, but there'll always be some that will listen to what we say.

I hope that this verse doesn't make you feel that if you're not literally weeping for someone's salvation, your prayers won't be effective. My spiritual passion isn't always released through tears, nor will yours be; sometimes our passion for people can be so deep that we are beyond weeping. He's the sympathetic Christ that sees deep into our souls and shares our heartache and passion for people we're trying to win.

King David was a man of passion. Do you know why he was "A man after God's own heart?" It was because David loved the Lord with all his heart—he had a passion for God, and he wasn't afraid to show that passion. I think many Christians are afraid to show any emotion or passion towards our Lord, but it's what Jesus desires from us.

Don't be afraid to cry tears. After all, didn't God create us with the ability to cry? Our tears represent our very soul, and we shouldn't try to suppress or ignore our emotions. Max Lucado writes; "To put a lock and key on your emotions is to bury part of your Christ likeness!"

"I believe that much of the secret of soul-winning lies in having bowels of compassion, in having spirits that can be touched with the feeling of human infirmities. Carve a preacher out of granite, and even if you give him an angel's tongue, he will convert nobody. Put him into the most fashionable pulpit, make his elocution faultless, and his matter profoundly orthodox, but so long as he bears within his bosom a hard heart he can never win a soul. Soul-saving requires a heart that beats hard against the ribs. It requires a soul full of the milk of human kindness. This is the chief natural qualification for a soul winner, which under God and blessed of him, will accomplish wonders."[20]

Mary of Bethany showed a deep love and emotion to our Lord. Pouring perfume on Jesus' feet and wiping them dry with her hair may seem an overly emotional act to some of us today, but it was a pure expression of love and adoration in her heart. We cannot do what Mary did, but we can show our love for our Lord by consistently making praise and worship a part of our lifestyle.

Many Christians think that worship is something that we just do in a church service, but it is more than that. Worship is a life-style. We need to integrate worship in every area of our lives—in giving of our time and money, sharing the love of God with a lost person, living out the fruit of the Spirit on a daily basis, being faithful to the church services. In other words, the Holy Spirit needs to have control over every aspect of our lives.

There's been a few times at work that I had to pray for God to give me a passion for my patients. Just recently I had an elderly patient that really tried my patience. Amelia was slowly dying of a bad respiratory disease and at times she was very hateful to the nurses. All of the nurses would do everything possible to make her comfortable, but her attitude would still be the same.

One day I noticed she was more sad and lonely than usual, so I just sat down with her, took a hold of her hand, and started to talk to her. Surprisingly, she opened up to me and started to talk about her life. She stated that she had a real hard marriage, had a husband that abused her, and now some of her children won't talk to her. So I could see why she was so bitter about life and acted so angry and hateful.

My heart went out to her as I tried to make her day a little more cheery. I knew she needed the Lord in her life so I prayed silently that God would give me the right words to say to her. There are many hurting, lonely people in the sphere of our little world of acquaintances—we just need to open our eyes as they are at our jobs, in our neighborhoods, in our churches, everywhere.

Amelia told me that she was of the Catholic faith and had been faithful to the church all her life. Many times she would ask the nursing staff to find her rosary beads that she lost in her bed or had dropped on the floor. How many times have I seen people trust in some object like a small idol, a picture, beads, etc. to protect them from evil and even take them to Heaven.

Unsaved people cling to worldly wisdom, a wisdom that will damn their eternal souls to Hell. Only true wisdom comes from above. I Corinthians 3:19 says, "For the wisdom of this world is foolishness with God." The Bible tells us that repentance and acceptance of Jesus as Savior is the beginning of true wisdom.

One Saturday my job called me to work, and even though I didn't want to go in, I just felt deep in my heart that there was a reason for it. And glory to God, I soon found that reason. I took care of Amelia again, and this time, instead of a bad attitude, she smiled and held out her hand to me.

I complimented her on a deep blue bed-jacket that she was wearing that brought out the pretty blue in her eyes. I have found that to establish a good rapport with your patients, you need to find something to compliment them on. You can always find something good in everyone you meet—you may have to look hard, but you will find something.

The day was fairly quiet, so I took advantage of this and spent extra time with her. Amelia was sitting up in a chair and reading a prayer book that she had brought from home. So I made a positive comment on the book, and then I asked her if she had the assurance in her heart that she was going to Heaven. She said, "Can anyone know for sure?" I told her that the Bible says we can have a "know-so" salvation.

I then asked her if I could show her the way to Heaven from the Bible. We read together I John 5:13 where it says we can *KNOW* for sure that we have eternal life. "These things have I written unto you that believe on the name of the Son of God; that ye may know that ye have eternal life, and that ye may believe on the name of the Son of God."

I like to use Ephesians 2:8, 9 when dealing with our Catholic friends because they combine faith and good works for salvation. "For by grace are ye saved through faith; and that not of yourselves: it is the gift of God. Not of works, lest any man should boast." I tried to make it very clear to her that she cannot be saved by trusting in her baptism and the church sacraments.

I said, "Amelia, I want you to notice the word, "Grace" in this verse. Do you have any idea what it means?" She said, "No." So I continued, "It's God's unmerited favor that He wants to give you. There's nothing in this world you can do on your own that will earn your way to Heaven. We just need to turn to Jesus in simple repentance, asking Him for forgiveness, and accept His wonderful gift of salvation. Jesus paid it all when He died on the cross of Calvary for your sins, and there's nothing we can add to that."

Sometimes we have to use simple illustrations to get our point across. I had a beautiful, expensive pen in my pocket, so I held it out to her, and said, "Amelia, if you want this pen, what do you have to do to get it?" She said, "I would just take it and say, thank-you." I said, "It's the same way with eternal life—we reach out our feeble hands, and take the free offer of salvation." I told her that's it's not a gift until we accept it for ourselves.

I then showed her Matthew 11:28 where it says, "Come unto me, all ye that labor and are heavy laden, and I will give you rest." I said, "Everyone is invited to come, not to a priest or a preacher, not to the sacraments, not to the church, but to Jesus alone for salvation."

I went on to explain, "God made salvation so easy that a child of five can understand it. Amelia, wouldn't you like to trust Jesus right now to save you and not trust anymore in the sacraments and rituals of the church?" She prayed the sinner's prayer and I could tell she meant it with all her heart. I truly believed she became a child of God that very day.

One of the nurses noticed a softening about her attitude since that day, so I had the chance to tell her that Amelia recently became a Christian, and that Christ made a difference in her life. I told her that the Lord can change the most hardened, bitter heart and turn that life into a new creation.

How does He change a heart that's full of sin? It's a mystery that we'll never understand this side of Heaven. The Holy Spirit that dwells in our hearts is very powerful. Listen to the words of Jesus in John 3: 8 where He compares the new birth to the sound of the wind, "The wind bloweth where it listeth, and thou hearest the sound thereof, but canst not tell whence it cometh, and whither it goeth: so is every one that is born of the Spirit."

I like how John MacArthur comments on this verse, and I quote him: "Jesus' point was that just as the wind cannot be controlled or understood by human beings but its effects can be witnessed, so also it is with the Holy Spirit. He cannot be controlled or understood, but the proof of His work is apparent. Where the Spirit works, there is undeniable and unmistakable evidence." In other words, true saving faith results in a life of obedience.

We need to refuse to be lukewarm in our approach to lost people. Even when they're hostile and unkind to us, we need to look beyond that attitude and see them as lost and bound for a Christless eternity. Remember that Jesus always looked beyond the surface of an individual and gazed directly into the heart. Be hot for the cause of Christ. May the verse in 2 Corinthians 5:14 be our motto for life, "For the love of Christ constraineth us;..."

God's heart aches over those who are lost. Seeking lost souls was the all-consuming passion of our Lord demonstrated in the parables of Luke 15. His heart not only aches, but He rejoices over those who are found. I urge you to read and meditate on this chapter and ask Him to reveal Jesus to you in its pages. I personally feel that how well we know Him is revealed by whether or not our hearts ache and rejoice like His heart.

Regarding soul winning, James Wilhoit writes, "We are pipes to carry His grace to others and not buckets content to hoard it. Grace comes to us, to go through us, to others." We need to ask ourselves, "Are we hoarding this blessed gospel all to ourselves?" We need to be like the Samaritan woman that became so excited about finding the Messiah that she couldn't wait to tell the whole village about that "Living Water" Jesus gave her.

God refers to Himself as the "Fountain of living waters" in Jeremiah 2:13, and He allows us the privilege of being dispensers of that living water. He has no feet but our feet, He has no hands but our hands, and He has no lips but our lips to proclaim the blessed gospel.

Go ahead—become a person of passion. Do you not realize that Jesus was so passionate about you that He went to the Cross and bore your sin and shame? If Jesus suffered our hell for us, then no sacrifice should ever be too great for us. Think about it—the very passion that sent Jesus to the Cross is also in you. We can literally have the same passion that Jesus had for lost souls.

May the words of the following hymn by Herbert G. Tovey sink deep into our souls:

"Give me a passion for souls, dear Lord,
A passion to save the lost;
O that Thy love were by all adored,
And welcomed at any cost.
How shall this passion for souls be mine? Lord,
make Thou the answer clear:
Help me to throw out the old Lifeline
To those who are struggling near.
Jesus, I long, I long to be winning Men who are lost,
and constantly sinning;
O may this hour be one of beginning,
The story of pardon to tell."

Chapter 21

WIN THEM, ONE-BY-ONE

"He who covets a soul, draws water from a fountain; but he who trains a soul winner digs a well from which thousands may drink to life eternal."
Charles Spurgeon.

The ministry of Jesus was largely one of personal soul winning. He had time for the multitudes, but He also took time for the individual. Just to name a few, He won Nicodemus, a man of authority in Jerusalem and a member of the great Sanhedrim. Christ entered the cursed city of Jericho and called Zacchaeus, the rich publican, to follow Him. Watch our compassionate Lord as He rescues the Gadarene demoniac out of the hands of Satan. All through the New Testament we see that the nearest thing to the heart of God was the winning of precious souls.

"Andrew...first findeth his own brother Simon....And he brought him to Jesus. Jesus would go forth into Galilee, and findeth Philip. Philip findeth Nathanael, and saith unto him, we have found Him..." (John 1:41-45).

We are not told that Andrew never preached a sermon, but the brother he brought to Jesus preached a sermon that led three thousand people to Jesus in one day. There wouldn't have been any great sermon if it had not been for Andrew's personal work. I'm convinced that the most important kind of Christian work is personal work. I admire some preachers that speak to large crowds, but there is tremendous power in personal soul winning.

Edward Kimball, a humble Sunday School teacher, obeyed the leading of the Holy Spirit and brought Dwight L. Moody to the Lord—just one. But that one was many because this famous evangelist shook two continents for God.

I have seen unsaved people go completely untouched from a church service, but days or even months may go by, and that person is reached by a personal soul winner. During a service, a preacher may not be able to meet the specific needs of an individual, whereas, in personal soul winning, quality time can be spent in answering questions and meeting the spiritual needs of that individual.

God has not called all of us to be preachers, foreign missionaries, or even Sunday school teachers, but there is not a child of God who cannot do personal work. Do you realize that God calls some people to work in the business world, some He's called to be schoolteachers, nurses, doctors, artists, etc.

God calls people in every profession to fill every niche of society and influence it with the gospel. Not everyone is going to go to a church to hear the gospel, nor will everyone listen to a Christian TV show, or read the Word of God. That's why God places Christians in places where they can saturate that area with the gospel.

He intends for us to fulfill the Great Commission wherever we are. You can obey Him by witnessing to a neighbor over a backyard fence, give a gospel tract to a grocery clerk, or witness to an unsaved person on an airline flight. Remember, you have the same power in you that Jesus has, and when we witness to someone, we are planting seeds of eternal life in their heart.

When I moved to Las Vegas, Nevada, I had the most wonderful neighbors in the world. Joe and Nema were always there for me and always willing to lend a helping hand. Ann and Jim, (my sister and brother-in-law) and I became very close friends with them, and in time, Nema started to go to church with us.

Nema had some hard knocks in life before we knew her. She carried a beautiful baby boy to full-term only to lose him at delivery. Due to the severe complications of the delivery, she almost hemorrhaged to death. Her marriage ended in divorce due to her husband's heavy drinking and infidelity; but, unbeknown to her, God was working behind the scenes and arranging things in her favor.

She soon developed a trusting friendship with someone that eventually became her husband. Joe was the kindest man she had ever met, and even though she vowed she would never marry again, love prevailed and they were soon married.

Right after her marriage to Joe she developed lymphoma and suffered with continuous treatments of chemotherapy and radiation. There were many times she wanted to give up due to the horrible side effects from chemotherapy, but she had a stubborn determination that someday she would be cured. At present, she is in remission, but to make matters worse, her doctor diagnosed her recently with chronic obstructive pulmonary disease. Due to this bad lung disease she is very prone to developing pneumonia.

There were a few times when she came very close to dying, but each time the Lord intervened in her life and healed her. Nema never became bitter during all these trials and never once did she question God. Oftentimes she would be discouraged, but she knew deep down that there was a purpose in living, and she soon found out what that purpose was.

One night as her and I were talking about spiritual matters, she shared with me that she had gone to a Baptist Church and was baptized as a child, but she did not have any peace in her heart. So I just gently asked her, "Nema, are you sure you are saved?"

She answered back, "No, I really don't think I am." Right there in my living room, I had the blessed privilege of showing her from God's Word that we can know beyond the shadow of a doubt that we can have eternal life.

That night, Nema trusted Jesus as her own personal Savior. Her destiny was changed forever and by God's unfailing grace she was forever sealed as a child of the King. It was such a joy to see her come to know my Lord and then to watch her grow spiritually.

About 2-3 months after Nema's conversion her husband was saved. Joe was raised Catholic, and was depending on his good works to save him. He was a very proud individual and God had to bring him through some tough times before he gave his heart to the Lord.

During his years of marriage to his first wife, Joe and his family lived in the lap of luxury. Joe was a self-made man that climbed the ladder of success to become a millionaire. With two beautiful three million dollar homes in California, a new, sporty Jaguar every year, a sixty-five foot yacht; he had anything money could buy. Then one day, disaster hit and God took everything away. After losing his only child to a drunken driver and losing his gorgeous wife to cancer, Joe became very bitter and depressed. Everything he loved and worked for was gone.

After his wife's funeral, and in a state of shock and grief, he left everything, and took a bus to Las Vegas with only fifty dollars in his pocket. He didn't care if he lived or died. At times he contemplated ending it all—there was nothing to live for now. The beautiful wife that was at one time "Miss Ohio" was gone forever. He had deeply loved his wife and daughter—life would never be the same. But, over time, he began to accept what happened to him and the bitterness gradually began to fade.

Just when life seemed to return to normal, more drama struck his life soon after marrying Nema. He developed cancer as a result of exposure to a chemical called "agent orange" while serving in Vietnam. After what seemed like an eternity of chemotherapy treatments, he is at present in remission and his prognosis remains good.

He would be very receptive when Jim would witness to him, and slowly, we saw his heart soften towards spiritual things. All his life he had been taught that salvation was by faith plus following all the rituals of the church. Jim gave him a little booklet that explained the difference between the "done religion" and the "do religion." Quoting the Word of God, it showed how following traditions and rituals couldn't save us, but our salvation rests completely on the finished work of Calvary.

He read this booklet when he was at home by himself one Sunday morning. All of a sudden the realization dawned upon him that he could not be saved by his own merits that he had been trusting in all his life. He acknowledged his sins and put his trust only in the shed blood of Jesus to save him. Joy flooded his heart because now he knew that his sins were forgiven and he had the sweet assurance of eternal life. He now had a hope and a peace that his religion never gave him.

Like many people, Joe had quite a bit of Biblical knowledge, but just having a head knowledge about Jesus never saved anyone; one needs to have a heart knowledge and a personal relationship with the Lord Jesus before he can ever enter Heaven's gates.

It's such a joy to see our friends come to know Jesus and then to see them grow in the things of God. Now, Joe studies his Bible with new vigor; the Bible is not just a textbook like it was before, because now, he knows the Author of the Book. That's what makes the difference!

Joe and Nema Riggi, my neighbors, Las Vegas, Nevada

God has a way of "melting frozen souls." Let me explain. Psalms 147:18 says, "He sendeth out his word, and melteth them; he causeth his wind to blow, and the waters flow." Joe wasn't even aware of it, but God was in the process of melting his stony, bitter heart towards spiritual things.

Matthew Henry sheds more light on this Scripture: "He sends out his word and melts them; the frost, the snow, the ice, are all dissolved quickly, in order to which he causes the wind, the south wind, to blow, and the waters, which were frozen, flow again as they did before. This thawing word may represent the gospel of Christ, and this thawing wind the Spirit of Christ (for the Spirit is compared to the wind, John 3:8); both are sent for the melting of frozen souls. Converting grace, like the thaw, softens the heart that was hard, moistens it, and melts it into tears of repentance; it warms good affections, and makes them to flow, which, before, were chilled and stopped up. It is very evident, and yet how it is done is unaccountable; such is the change wrought in the conversion of a soul, when God's Word and Spirit are sent to melt it and restore it to itself."[21]

Joe and Nema have a place at the military base here in Las Vegas where they sell their "World of Products." They have a gospel tract ministry where they offer a tract to their customers. I get so blessed when I see them do this because one sign that a person is genuinely saved is the burden they have for the unsaved. And, as a result of their Christian testimony and concern for others, their close neighbors are coming faithfully to church.

Nema knows her mission in life—to see the members of her beloved family saved. Every week she faithfully picks up her nieces and nephews for church, and just recently her nephew was saved. This is what the Christian life is all about—winning them, one by one. The late Dr. Adrian Rogers made a very simple, but profound statement regarding this: "There's something better than going to Heaven—it's taking someone with you!" Nema has truly taken that to heart, and she won't rest until all of her family members are saved.

My friend, we are commanded to win them one-by-one. Hudson Taylor, the great missionary to China, stated, "The Great Commission is not an option to be considered; it is a command to be obeyed." If you are part of the family of God, your mission is mandatory. To ignore it would be sheer disobedience. Always remember that with the enlightenment or knowledge that God gives you comes responsibility in sharing it with a lost world.

Chapter 22

RELIGIOUS, BUT LOST

"Right now we are in an age of religious complicity. The simplicity, which is in Christ, is rarely found among us. In its stead are programs, methods, organizations and a world of nervous activities which occupy time and attention but can never satisfy the longing of the heart."
A.W. Tozer

There are millions of religious people in this world. It is a fact that God placed within every man the desire to worship something, whether it is himself, an idol made of stone, or the true and living God. Man is a religious being whether he knows it or not. He was made to worship something.

Within man is a God-shaped vacuum that can only be filled with the Creator, Himself. It is such an awesome thing to know that God made us with a spiritual capacity to really know and love Him. What people need is found in a person, the person of the Lord Jesus Christ, not in religion. Religion is just another futile attempt to reach God by trying to be good. Jesus is the life of God in us, and no human being will ever achieve this life without Him.

Whenever the Lord gives me an opportunity to witness, I always think of the beautiful passage found in John 7:37,

38. "If any man thirst, let him come unto me and drink. He that believeth on me, as the scripture hath said, out of his belly shall flow rivers of living water." Jesus explained the Holy Spirit in our lives by using the image of a strong river of water flowing out of us. Rivers of water is the way Jesus describes the normal life of believers.

Sarah was a beautiful lady in her late fifties when I knew her. She was my surgical patient for about two weeks in a hospital in Spokane, Washington. This dear lady was a prime example of a very religious person who went to church all her life, participated in praise and worship, very active in the programs of the church, but lost without the Savior.

When I took care of her she couldn't brag enough on her church and the minister. But all the time she talked to me I never heard how wonderful Jesus was to her. After listening to her I just simply asked her, "Sarah, when were you saved?" She looked at me real funny and said, "Well, I've always been saved—my mother had me in church when I was only four days old and I've been going ever since."

I gently explained to her that we need to experience the "New birth" in order to go to Heaven. She looked real puzzled and asked, "What is the new birth?"

I gave her the following illustration: "We can liken the spiritual birth to our physical birth. There has to be a specific time and place when we were born physically, and the spiritual birth is the same way. We aren't born automatically into God's Kingdom."

She then said, "My preacher has never told us about this. Are you sure it's in the Bible?"

I replied, "Sarah, let me tell you how a person can have this new birth. It's found in John 3. Because man is born a fallen, sinful creature, he must be born again by the Spirit of God before he can see the Kingdom of God." I read her the wonderful verses in this chapter, and then gave her my testimony of how the Lord saved me.

I knew that Sarah went to a Unitarian Church where they believe that man was born basically good, not with the sinful nature that the Bible tells us we have. They also reject the traditional doctrines of the Virgin Birth, The Trinity, Hell, and the Atoning death of Jesus. So, knowing what her church taught her, I knew that she had probably never heard a clear presentation of the gospel.

Sarah did not get saved when I had her as a patient, but I could tell she was still interested in spiritual things. Before she was discharged from the hospital she asked me for my phone number and said she would like to keep in touch. So I was delighted to give it to her and prayed that the Holy Spirit would work in her heart.

A week after I discharged her she was re-admitted to the hospital due to a bad infection from her surgery. Even though I hated to see her suffer from the infection, I couldn't help but wonder if it was for a reason. She stayed on my unit for a week with intravenous antibiotics, and during that time we got to know each other better and I was able to answer her questions about Biblical issues.

Some time after she went home from the hospital I met her for lunch. She said to me, "I've read everything you gave me, but I'm having a real hard time believing in a place called Hell. I've always believed that God is a good God, and He is too good to let anyone go to this terrible place."

That afternoon we poured over the Scriptures concerning this subject and I could tell the Holy Spirit was opening her heart to the truths of God's Word. I showed her many passages regarding this subject, some of which were Mark 16:16, Psalm 9:17, Luke 16:19-31, and Revelation 20:11-15. What a joy it was to see her interest in spiritual things. Sarah promised to attend my church the following Sunday.

After she came to my church for about three weeks, my pastor's wife and I went to her home on a visitation night, and before we left Sarah became a Christian. What a blessed time of fellowship we had that day with this dear lady. Two weeks later my minister baptized her and she joined our church.

I wonder how many people sit Sunday after Sunday in churches and leave unsaved. They think that they're doing God a favor by going to church and that He'll smile on their religious works. And I know that this also happens in our fundamental churches. I have learned over the years that we should not be so presumptuous as to assume that everybody who goes to church is truly saved.

Sarah told me later that she was praying and witnessing to her children. That really sent a thrill through my heart because I believe that when a person is truly saved, then there will be a burden for other people, especially those in their own family. I love the old saying, "True saving faith results in a life of obedience."

I often think of the passage in Luke 12:48 where it speaks about the parable of the faithful steward. Listen to these words of Jesus: "For unto whomsoever much is given, of him shall be much required." We cannot live for ourselves anymore because we have been given too much knowledge for that. God has entrusted each of us with a valuable treasure—a lifetime of opportunities, and some day, we will be judged on what we did with those opportunities.

"We can prove our faith by our committal to it, and in no other way. Any faith that does not command the one who holds it is not a real belief; it is a pseudo belief only. And it might shock some of us profoundly if we were brought suddenly face to face with our beliefs and forced to test them in the fires of practical living.

"Many of us Christians have become extremely skillful in arranging our lives so as to admit the truth of Christianity without being embarrassed by its implications.

"So wide is the gulf that separates theory from practice in the church that an inquiring stranger who chances upon both would scarcely dream that there was any relation between them. An intelligent observer of our human scene who heard the Sunday morning sermon, and later watched the Sunday afternoon conduct of those who had heard it, would conclude that he had been examining two distinct and contrary religions.

"Christians habitually weep and pray over beautiful truth, only to draw back from that same truth when it comes to the difficult job of putting it in practice."[22]

Chapter 23

THE URGENCY OF OUR MISSION

*You may be someone's last warning signal
before they enter eternity.*

Imagine that Jesus is among us in person. "Come close." You move closer to Him, straining to drink in every word He says. You gaze on Him with rapturous wonder, never taking your eyes off His dear face. Then, without warning, Jesus is taken up in the clouds out of your sight. You stand there, eyes straining to catch the last glimpse of Him, wishing with all your heart He would return.

You know that you'll remember every word He said for the rest of your life. How you would ponder those last words over and over again until you knew them by heart. And you would not forget the way He looked at you with compassionate eyes, and how you would long to hear that voice again.

Now, you've just caught a glimpse of what the disciples encountered in Acts 1:8-11. They have followed Jesus for three years, believing He was truly the Messiah—the One worth risking everything to follow. Now, they were standing on the Mount of Olives, listening to His very last words before He ascended up into Heaven.

Listen carefully – "But ye shall receive power, after that the Holy Ghost is come upon you; and ye shall be witnesses unto me both in Jerusalem, and in all Judea, and in Samaria, and unto the uttermost part of the earth." Should we not cherish and obey the last words of our Lord? Is He not also precious to us?

I've heard some Christians say that we are to witness to others by our "Christian life-style" (called "Life-style Evangelism"). They say that we're not supposed to go around trying to persuade others to accept Christ because that might offend them. So, they do nothing. I have been very guilty of this very thing.

Yes, we are to live a life based on Christian principles, but that is not enough, The word, "Witness," means to "Open your mouth and testify." We are to give evidence of Christ in our lives by giving out the plan of salvation, and at the same time, back this up with a godly life. We shouldn't witness to an unsaved person about Christ if there's blatant sin in our lives.

I can vividly remember taking care of a man that had terminal lung cancer. The doctor gave him six months to live, so I thought I had plenty of time to witness to him. Was I ever wrong! He was alert, up in his wheel chair, went to the various activities, and just didn't act like a terminally ill patient.

I took care of him for three weeks, came back to work after having five days off, and found him with pneumonia. The night nurse reported to me that he developed it very quickly and would not respond to intravenous antibiotics. He was unresponsive and I knew that his days were numbered.

What a blow that was to me and how the Holy Spirit convicted me of the sin of procrastination. Oh, yes, I had asked him earlier if he would like a minister to visit him, but I never shared Christ with him. I tried to appease myself, thinking maybe he had heard the gospel before; surely with all the Christians in the world, and all the Christian TV shows, he had a chance to hear the gospel and be saved, but the Holy Spirit would not give me any peace. I knew that I was probably the last Christian he saw, and I blew it.

I can remember during those first three weeks the Holy Spirit nudged me several times to give him a gospel tract to read, and each time I was distracted from doing it. As I look back, those distractions weren't even that important. Satan is very clever and he will throw all kinds of diversions in our path. He would rather have you do anything besides share your faith—he'll encourage you to do all kinds of good deeds as long as you don't try to take anyone to Heaven with you.

I've let this experience be a lesson to me to never take for granted that I always have "tomorrow" to witness to a lost person. Life is very fragile and we never know what a day will bring forth. I can't over-emphasize the urgency of our mission. We must not keep silent about Jesus. The cost of such silence is too high for those people waiting to hear.

Keeping our witness silent is in actuality denying Christ. We think badly of Peter when he denied Christ before the crucifixion, but we do the very same thing when we know we should open our mouths and we keep silent. Some classic excuses of this might include: "I'm too busy." "I don't know what to say." "I don't have the gift of evangelism." "I fear rejection." "People would not want to listen to me." Always remember that to be silent about our wonderful Savior and His salvation is a dreadful sin of omission.

We need to see the big picture of our lives. We are bought with a price; the precious blood of Christ, and our goal in life should not be to live for ourselves, but to bring glory and honor to our Savior. We bring Him glory when we live godly lives that leave an impact on the unsaved world. Jesus is not playing games with us. Either we believe and follow Him, or we throw our Bible away, and live for ourselves. There is no middle ground. If we truly believe what we say, then, let's be different. There's an old proverb that says, "We only truly believe that which motivates us to action."

Each of us lives in a different world—we go in different paths every day and are around different people. Have you ever wondered why that is? It's because God places you around people that only you can win. They'll listen to you where they may never listen to anyone else.

I remember working with a certain young nurse three years ago that I only knew for one day. She was new on the job, and it was my job to orient her. Our lunchtime was at the same time so we ate together in the lunchroom. As my custom, I simply bowed my head and silently gave thanks for the food before I ate. She then asked if I was a Christian and the conversation was turned into spiritual avenues.

She shared with me that she had never been to a church service, but had been recently listening to a TV evangelist and had been seriously thinking about what he was saying. I told her that it was no accident that God brought this preacher into her life. She said to me in a surprised voice, "Well, what do you mean?"

I replied, "God brings certain people into our lives for a purpose, and in this instance it was so you could hear the gospel and be saved. We should respond to the gospel the first time we hear it because we may not have another chance."

Before we left the lunch table I gave her my testimony of how the Lord saved me and changed my life. I gave her a gospel tract with the title, *"Where will you spend Eternity?"* and encouraged her to accept Jesus into her life. She thanked me and said she would read it. Before we parted ways that day I told her I'd be praying for her.

The following week I received word that she had been instantly killed in a horrible car accident. She was not wearing her seat belt, and the impact of the crash ejected her through the windshield some one hundred feet. The news saddened me because I never knew if she had trusted Christ as her personal Savior, but I was so glad that I had the chance to talk with her about the Lord. I can only hope that she is in Heaven.

Don't tell me that it was just a coincidence that I worked with Pat that day. God brings people into our life for an hour—a day—a month—a year—for a reason. After this incident, I couldn't get her off my mind. It made me seriously think of how our lives affect other people every day. If we could draw back the curtain and get a glimpse into eternity, and see the glorious bliss of the believer and the miseries of the lost, oh, what a difference it would make in our conduct here.

Opportunities stare us in the face every day. Bruce Wilkinson calls them "Divine Appointments," and that's exactly what they are. If we don't have eternity stamped in our hearts for those God brings into our paths, then, we will not see them as divine interventions, and we will miss out on the wonderful blessing God has for us.

While writing this chapter, God brought into my path a twenty-year-old college student who was working for Wal-Mart. He was working in the parking lot near my car, and as I was putting groceries in my car he asked if he could help. After he was done helping me, I asked him if I could give him something special to read on his lunch break. He took the gospel tract I gave him, looked down at it, then looked real strange at me and said, "You know, it's real funny that you gave me this, because I've been thinking real seriously about going back to church." He then went on to say, "My mother died recently of cancer, and her Christian life left a big impact on my life."

I replied back, "It would make your mother very happy if she knew that you were obeying the Lord." He said, "I was saved as a child, but wandered away from God in my teen years. I know I'm out of fellowship with the Lord and sometimes I feel a 'tugging' in my heart."

I told him, "That 'tugging' is the convicting power of the Holy Spirit urging you to get your heart right with the Lord." I'll probably never see this young man again, but I truly believe that God brought him into my path to encourage him in the things of the Lord. We should always be proactive, always on the lookout for opportunities. Be sensitive and pay attention to the people around you. When we ask God to bless us with divine appointments, then, our faith is activated, which opens the door for Him to work in our life.

I recall taking care of an elderly lady that developed pneumonia. She was a very frail patient that had a long history of heart problems. I always try to make rounds on my patients every two hours, and as I came to her bedside I saw tears in her eyes. I sat down beside her, took her hand in mine, and asked her why she was crying. She said, "I'm so frightened that I'm going to die." I took advantage of this opportunity to ask her if she was ready to die. She said, "No, I really don't think I am."

I then asked her if I could show her the way to Heaven from the Bible. After I did this, she asked me, "Are you a Catholic?"

I said, "No, but every verse I showed you from my New Testament is in your own Catholic Bible." After I said that, she was very eager to be saved. I said, "Wanda, are you willing to put your trust only in the precious blood of Jesus to save you, and let go of all the church rituals and your baptism to save you?"

She answered back, "Yes, I will." I then showed her Scriptures on how the grace of God works in our hearts, bringing us to repentance.

What she said really blessed my heart. "I know my Bible is true, and if God said it, then I believe it." I made sure she understood the plan of salvation, and that day she very sweetly trusted Christ as her Savior.

"When we seek God's blessing as the ultimate value in life, we are throwing ourselves entirely into the river of His will and power and purposes for us. You're praying for exactly what God desires. Suddenly, the unhindered forces of heaven can begin to accomplish God's perfect will—through you. He knows something you can't possibly know—every single person who's in desperate need of receiving His touch through you. God will bring you to that person at exactly the right time and in the right circumstances."[23]

One day, each of us will die, and eternity will open before us. We will take our last look here on earth and all the opportunities that God has given us will be forever gone. We should start viewing things now, as we will then. I urge you today to look around for a lonely person and extend your hand of mercy to that one that God has placed in your path.

The two most tragic regrets in eternity will be: (1) To have heard the gospel and rejected the Savior, and (2) To know Jesus as our personal Savior and never tried to win another to Him. My prayer is that each of us would become a beacon of light to those that cross our path that need the Savior.

Chapter 24

THE HEAVENLY WEDDING

We shall soon feast our eyes upon Him—the King in His beauty. What a heart-thriller that will be! We see a dazzling sunset and our hearts rejoice, but there is no comparison with the beauty of our Lord.

Everyone likes a good, romantic story. Well, the best love story I have ever read is found in our precious Bible, the book of Song of Solomon. It shows in beautiful parables how Christ, the royal Bridegroom, expresses His great love for His mystic bride, the church. And the bride expresses her great delight in Him, and the dearest desire of her heart is to commune with Him.

The Lord Jesus Christ has many wonderful names in this tiny book. The sweetest and the most beautiful names *are The Rose of Sharon* and *The Lily of the Valley*. Have you ever wondered why that is?

Let's take the rose, the chief of all flowers, is known for its breath-taking beauty and heavenly fragrance. One word to describe it is "splendid." And, the rose has a message for all: When the rosebud opens up, this denotes that the wonderful gospel lies open to all—no one is excluded. He is not a rose that can be locked up in a garden, but His fragrance reaches throughout the entire world.

Look very carefully at the lily of the valley flower. This flower has white bell-shaped flowers and it bears fruit of scarlet berries. The flower stands for chastity, purity, sweetness, and humility. Spiritually, the red berries symbolize His precious blood that was shed for us. What a beautiful picture this book paints of our Beloved, the Lord Jesus Christ!

We see the bride meditating on her Bridegroom in Chapters 2 & 7: "The voice of my beloved! Behold, He cometh leaping upon the mountains, skipping upon the hills...I am my beloved's, and his desire is toward me." The bride is comforted when she thinks about the relationship between her and her Bridegroom. She is His forever and all the glorious things He has prepared in Heaven belong to her. In Heaven our desires are crowned with unspeakable delights. All our sorrows and griefs will have vanished and all our joy will be centered in God.

Even though the bride is in love with her Bridegroom, she still has that old fallen nature within her, and she will not be rid of it until she is in Heaven with her Beloved. The picture changes to a melancholy scene in Chapter 5. We see the bride telling about her unfaithfulness and listlessness to her lover—she slept when she should have been communing with Him. There was a coolness in her attitude and she was neglectful of her duties towards Him.

She had let worldly desires interrupt her relationship with her Beloved. These are described as "The foxes, the little foxes that spoil the vines..." (Chapter 2:15). We need to be always aware of creeping, small sins that like to grow and defile us.

Oh, listen to the sobbing bride, "I opened to my beloved, but my beloved had withdrawn himself, and was gone; my soul failed when he spake: I sought him, but I could not find him; I called him, but he gave me no answer." (Chapter 5:6). The bride finds that when she neglects the sweet place of prayer or the call of God upon her life, then she may find the sweet fellowship she once had with him gone. With anguished heart, she seeks to find Him. The night surrounds her and fears are on every side—she wades through pools of tears before she finds Him.

But listen—what does the bride hear? "My heart waketh, it is the voice of my Beloved that knocketh, saying, open to me, my sister, my love, my dove, my undefiled." (Chapter 5:2). He calls her, "My dove," a metaphor that expresses tenderness and gentleness. Although we are unworthy and defiled by sin, yet, when we come to Christ, we are made beautiful.

How gracious our Lord is to us. Even though we may wander away from Him, He brings us back in His presence. Those whom He loves He will not let alone in their carelessness, but will find a way to awaken them out of their spiritual lethargy.

He knocks to awaken us to come and let Him in, and sometimes He has to resort to intense pain to bring us to our senses. Pain—everyone hates it, but it is a sure way of getting our attention. I like to call it God's megaphone. It is not punishment, but it is a wake-up call to arouse us from our disobedience. He loves us too much to let us wander in our wayward ways.

I like what C.S. Lewis says, "God whispers through pleasure but shouts through pain. Sometimes our Heavenly Father has to shout." God is not mad at us—instead He's mad about us and He'll do whatever it takes to bring us back into fellowship with Him.

Do you realize that God is very jealous of you? He has a passionate, consuming zeal for our best interests. Getting to know Him as a jealous God will increase our level of devotion to Him, and will strengthen our dedication to faithfully share His truth with others.

Oh, if we could only learn that when we are out of fellowship with our Savior, then we forfeit His choicest secrets and blessings in our lives. We need to be quick to hear and respond to the voice of our Heavenly Bridegroom, for He wants nothing but the best for His children.

Hear the voice of the bride again as she pleads with Him to have a more intimate communion with Him. "Set me as a seal upon thy heart, as a seal upon thy arm:…" (Chapter 8:6). In other words, she desires to have her name written on His heart and to be comforted by having His everlasting arms wrapped around her.

"He brought me to the banqueting house, and his banner over me was love" (Chapter 2:4). Many Christians fail to feed their empty souls—instead, they feed upon the glamour and junk of this world. They stand like an outsider, like a homeless child, peering into the window of a great mansion as a great feast is taking place within. Their stomachs grumble in hunger as they see the roast lamb being sliced and they see the juices seeping over the meat. What do they fail to see?—an empty seat reserved with their name on it.

If you are truly saved, you are a part of God's great royal family. You are invited to "Come and Dine" at your Father's banqueting table. Don't stare through the window. Go in and take your seat where you belong—you're a child of the King. He's waiting for you with loving arms that long to embrace you.

Note again the precious privilege of the bride in Chapter 2:14 where she is said to be "In the secret place of the stairs,…" This would speak of access to our Beloved. This truth should make our hearts burst with joy, because now we have the privilege of ascending to the Father by actually coming boldly into that glorious throne room with all our burdens and intercessions. We don't have to go through a priest or a preacher—we are privileged to go directly to our Bridegroom with our confessions and intercessions for others.

The Song of Solomon ends with the Bridegroom departing for just a while to the "Mountains of Spices" in Heaven where He is preparing mansions of delight for His bride. She must stay below in the "Gardens on earth" where she has work to do for Him. She desires His speedy return to her. "Make haste, my Beloved, and be thou like to a roe or to a young hart upon the mountains of spices" (Chapter 8:14). Even so, come, Lord Jesus, come quickly!

Oh, what a dear and glorious Savior we have—can we ever read about our Beloved without having deep emotion and adoring gratitude? I love the writing of Bernard of Clair Vaux, "The love of Jesus, what it is, none but His loved ones know." And this is so true—people that reject Him will never taste of the continual joy of really knowing Him.

"You cannot with your utmost stretch of imagination conceive the beauty which now adorns our King; yet, brethren, there will be a further revelation of it when He shall appear in His glory, for He is yet to descend from Heaven in great power....Jesus wears all the beauty which the pomp of Heaven can bestow upon Him, all the glory which ten thousand times ten thousand angels can minister to Him. Jesus is in the midst of them as in the holy place." Charles Spurgeon.

The most thrilling experience for all believers will be when Jesus comes again to take us to be with Him for evermore, called the Rapture of the Church. This blessed event is described in I Thessalonians 4:13-17. After we are raptured to our Heavenly Home we will be presented to Him as His radiant bride at the Marriage Supper of the Lamb. Our heavenly marriage will finally be consummated—we will become eternally one with the Lord Jesus Christ.

Revelation 19:7, 8 tells us, "Let us be glad and rejoice, and give honour to him; for the marriage of the Lamb is come, and his wife hath made herself ready. And to her was granted that she should be arrayed in fine linen, clean and white..." After the wedding, we will have a glorious honeymoon that will last a thousand years in the Millennium. Yet that is only the beginning. What joy and ecstasy awaits us!

> *The Father*
> *Requests the honour of your presence*
> *At the marriage supper of His Son*
> *Jesus Christ*
> *To be held in Heaven*
> *Only those will be admitted*
> *Who come clothed in the Wedding Garment*
> *Provided by the Father*
> *"For He hath clothed me with the garments of salvation,*
> *He hath covered me with the robe of righteousness."*
> *Isaiah 61:10*

Maybe I'm addressing an unsaved person who has never accepted this invitation to this wonderful wedding. This particular wedding requires the proper clothing, which is spotless and clean. Sin keeps us from a right relationship with God, but Jesus provided a way that we can be clothed in His righteousness. "The blood of Jesus Christ, his Son cleanseth from all sin" (1 John 1:7).

Jesus gives His last invitation to sinners in Revelation 22:17. "And the Spirit and the bride say, Come. And let him that heareth say, Come. And let him that is athirst come. And whosoever will, let him take the water of life freely." My friend, "whosoever" means you—you do not want to miss this grand and glorious wedding.

God has so graciously given you this very moment to repent and turn to the Savior. Then, you can rejoice in the fact that your name is written in the Lamb's Book of Life, and you'll be able to say with all assurance that "I am my beloved's, and my beloved is mine:..." (Song of Solomon 6:3).

Chapter 25

THE CROWN OF REJOICING

The main goal in our lives should be to hear our dear Savior personally say to us, "...Well done, thou good and faithful servant..."(Matthew 25:21).

In the previous chapter, we saw where the bride is forever with her Beloved Bridegroom, and what a glorious day that will be. Following the Rapture, believers will be brought to the Bema Seat, or called The Judgment Seat of Christ, where everyone will give an account of himself to God. We will not be judged for our sins as that was taken care of at Calvary, but believers will be rewarded according to their faithful stewardship.

Do you know that there will be embarrassment on that great judgment day? Many believers have been deceived in thinking that once they have a free ticket to Heaven, they can relax and sin all they want. As a result, they will have to stand shame-faced, watching their works be destroyed.

Salvation is about more than just getting to Heaven. Anyone who is an avid follower of Jesus knows that we do not get away with sin. Every unconfessed sin will be examined. But on the other hand, we have the sweet assurance that none of our good works will go unnoticed.

We need to realize that there is no way for a Christian to escape the Judgment Seat of Christ. Paul tells us in 2 Corinthians 5:10, "For we must all appear before the judgment seat of Christ;..." And what is the purpose? "That everyone may receive the things done in his body, according to that he hath done, ...whether it be good or bad." Every believer, from the day of conversion, should strive to win souls for Christ. The Scripture reminds us that we are co-laborers with God.

Rewards in Scripture are given in the form of crowns. Our Heavenly Father is so good to us. To think that He wants to reward us fallen creatures—sinners, saved by grace; and to know that after we receive these crowns, we get the happy privilege of casting them at the feet of Jesus. We will be crying from the depths of our hearts, "Thou, art worthy, O Lord, to receive glory and honor and power:..." (Revelation 4:11).

Keep in mind that receiving a reward (I like to call it, our final "paycheck") should not be our motivation for serving the Lord. But we will find joy in thinking about Heaven and our rewards as we serve our Heavenly Father in love. If love is not our motivation for service, then, the Bible says our works will be burned up.

The Bible tells us that there are five crowns that are available to every believer. In this chapter we will only address one of them. The Bible also tells us that we should be very careful that someone else does not receive the crown that was intended for us.

This Crown of Rejoicing is also called the "Soul Winner's Crown." If anyone deserves this crown, it is the Apostle Paul. Listen to him describe this particular crown in I Thessalonians 2:19, "For what is our hope, or joy, or crown of rejoicing? Are not even ye in the presence of our Lord Jesus Christ at His coming?" What is Paul talking about? He is saying that this is the crown that you receive because you led someone to Christ. It's the crown that God gives to His children when they stop thinking "It's all about me" and reach out to people that need a touch from God.

"Joy" stands out in my mind regarding this crown. Whenever we read about soul winning, there is always joy attached to it. But we always need to remember that Satan wants to rob us of our joy and crown, and He'll do everything He can to paralyze our attempts at winning souls to the Savior. We must not let the adversary hinder our efforts in being a blessing to countless people that are lost in sin.

Are you aware that there will be tears in Heaven? We will weep over lost opportunities and our failure to win the lost around us. If we have let loved ones go unwarned to Hell, no matter how sorry we are and how graciously we are forgiven, the fact remains that they are still lost. When this reward is passed out, the Bible says that we will suffer loss. However, God, with His own kind hand, will wipe away our tears, and we will have the sweet assurance that we will be forever finished with sorrow and crying.

Let's assume that you are standing at the Judgment Seat of Christ, and you have been neglectful about your responsibility of winning souls. When the time came for you to worship Christ with this Crown, you will have to stand aside and watch others receive it with joy. Can there be any greater regret than this? Wouldn't you rather experience an eternity of joy enhanced by the knowledge that people are in Heaven because you were that instrument that God used in bringing souls to the Savior?

In 1877, the Rev. A. G. Upham tells the story of a young man who was about to die. He'd only been a Christian for a month, and was sad because he'd had so little time to serve the Lord. He made the comment that he wasn't afraid to die because the Lord saved him, but his dying words were, "Must I go, and empty-handed." A man by the name of Charles C.

Luther heard this story, and it was this incident that prompted him to write the following hymn:

"Must I go, and empty-handed,
Thus my dear Redeemer meet?
Not one day of service bring Him;
Lay no trophy at His feet?

Oh the years in sinning wasted,
Could I but recall them now,
I would give them to my Saviour;
To His will I'd gladly bow.

Oh ye saints, arouse, be earnest,
Up and work while yet 'tis day;
Ere the night of death o'er-take thee,
Strive for souls while still you may.

Must I go, and empty-handed? Must I meet my Saviour so?
Not one soul with which to greet Him:
Must I empty-handed go?"

ENDNOTES

1. Charles H. Spurgeon, a sermon entitled, *Soul Winning*.

2. J. Sidlow Baxter, *Awake My Heart,* (Michigan: Zondervan Publishing, 1960), 225.

3. Max Lucado, *Come Thirsty*, (Tennessee: Thomas Nelson, 2006), 1.

4. J. Sidlow Baxter, *Going Deeper,* (Michigan: Zondervan Publishing, 1959), 184.

5. Creation Moments, a sermon entitled, *Disproving the Doubters*.

6. Paula R. Hartz, *Native American Religions,* (Brown Publishing Network, 1997).

7. J. Sidlow Baxter, *Awake My Heart,* (Michigan: Zondervan Publishing, 1960), 66.

8. J. Sidlow Baxter, *Awake My Heart,* (Michigan: Zondervan Publishing, 1960), 183.

9. J. Sidlow Baxter, *Awake My Heart,* (Michigan: Zondervan Publishing, 1960), 204.

10. J. Sidlow Baxter, *Awake My Heart*, (Michigan: Publishing, 1960), 30.

11. A. W. Tozer, *The Root of the Righteous*, (WingSpread, 1986), Chapter 2.

12. Matthew Henry, *Matthew Henry's Commentary*, (Michigan: Zondervan, 1960), 1974.

13. Oswald Chambers, *If You Will Ask*, (Michigan: Discovery House, 1961), 102-103.

14. Oswald Chambers, *If You Will Ask*, (Michigan: Discovery House, 1961), 103-104.

15. Dr. R. A. Torrey, a sermon entitled, *The Importance of Personal Winning*.

16. John Newton, *Out of the Depths,* (Kregel Publications, 2003).

17. David B. Crabtree, *There's Hope For Today,* (Book of Hope International, 2002).

18. Dr. R. A. Torrey, a sermon entitled, *The Importance of Soul Winning*.

19. J. Sidlow Baxter, *Awake My Heart,* (Michigan: Zondervan Publishing, 1960), 58.

20. Charles H. Spurgeon, a sermon entitled, *Soul Winning*.

21. Matthew Henry, *Matthew Henry's Commentary,* (Michigan: Zondervan, 1960), 730.

22. A. W. Tozer, *The Root of the Righteous*, (WingSpread, 1986), Chapter 13.

23. Bruce Wilkinson, *The Prayer of Jabez,* (Oregon: Multnomah Publishers, 2000), 24, 25, 83.

Breinigsville, PA USA
22 February 2010
232970BV00002B/2/P